# INTERCESSION THE HEART BEAT OF GOD

Catrina J. Sparkman

# INTERCESSION
# THE HEART BEAT OF GOD

Copyright © 2018 Catrina Sparkman
**ISBN 13: 978-1-949958-09-6**

All rights reserved. No part of this book may be reproduced, stored in whole or in part, or transmitted in any form or by any means, without prior written permission from the publisher, except in the case of brief quotations embodied in articles for review. Nor can this book be circulated in any form of binding or cover other than that in which it is published.

All Bible Scriptures taken from the following translations: New International Standard Version, God's Word Translation, English Standard Version, and The King James Version.

**Other Books by Catrina J. Sparkman**

## Non Fiction

*Doing Business with God*

*Intimacy the Beginning of Authority*

*Divine Revelation for a Twitter Generation*

*Doing Battle with the Name of the Lord*

*Wired for War*

## Fiction:

The Redemption's Price Series:

*Passing through Water*

*Opening the Floodgates*

*The Fire This Time*

# Table of Contents

Author's Note 1

Chapter 1: Prayer: A Revolutionary Act 4

Chapter 2: Standing in the Gap 19

Chapter 3: Repairing the Breeches 30

Chapter 4: The Press 40

Chapter 5: Backlash & Retaliation 58

Chapter 6: Avengers & Redeemers 66

Chapter 7: The Role of the Intercessor 76

Chapter 8: Governmental Intercession 118

Chapter 9: Intimacy & Authority 140

An Invitation to the Family of God 149

# Author's Note

I've always wanted to commission an artist to paint a portrait of the Army of God. I think that if someone were to paint this picture of God's mighty prayer army arising, you'd see mamas pushing strollers, babies with rattles in their hands. You'd see little old ladies with false teeth in their mouths. You'd see the outcast and the castaways. You'd see those who have been written off by society, as not being able to contribute anything of value. You'd see ex-prostitutes, ex-pimps, and ex-addicts, because when God was looking for a man to stand in the gap and make up the hedge— these were the ones who answered the call.

This book came about from a class I created many years ago, entitled *The Role of the Intercessor*. The purpose of the class was to take its participants through the Word of God from Genesis to Revelation and investigate what the Bible has to say regarding the ministry of intercession.

In the early days of the class, I would jokingly lead the people through finger exercises, in preparation for all the flipping through their Bibles that they would have to do. In this updated self-study on prayer you won't have to do that. I've done all the heavy lifting for you. I've printed just about every scripture referenced in the book right here on the pages.

In these chapters you will learn important warfare tools and some commonly held misconceptions about intercession. Together we will explore themes such as: the role of the prophet during corporate intercession, the role of the watchman who stands at the gate, and what happens in the unseen realms when we pray. It is my sincere prayer that as you engage in this study, you will learn God's expectations for humanity and why intercession really is the heartbeat of God.

In His Service,

Catrina J. Sparkman

# INTERCESSION
# The Heart Beat of God
## Part I

**Prayer: A Revolutionary Act**

**Standing in the Gap**

**Repairing the Breaches**

# CHAPTER ONE
# PRAYER: A REVOLUTIONARY ACT

Slavery has existed for every people group on every part of the planet. So black people don't have a monopoly on slavery, but slavery in the US was a much crueler type of system. In other places where slavery existed, say for instance, the Islands, slaves, if they felt they were being treated unusually harsh, could take their masters to court and lay claim against them. This was not the case for the enslaved Africans who were brought to America. Based on American law, they were not considered to be fully human, and so therefore could not lay claim to the legal rights of a human in a court of law.

One of the things that American slaves were not allowed to do was pray. There was something about the desperate quality of the enslaved Africans' prayers that caused them to be seen as a threat to the very establishment of slavery. These slaves, who could find no justice in the American legal system, would literally dig trenches in the ground and pour out the anguish that was deep within their souls to the only one who could intervene. This God called, Jehovah, that they had discovered across the waters.

I have no doubt in my mind that this was a prophetic act. Someone caught a revelation about planting their prayers inside the Earth and they began to trust God for a harvest. If the slaves were found praying in this way—with this desperate type of pressing prayer, then they would be beaten. If they were discovered praying in this fashion again, they would be sold. So, believe me when I say there was a very big incentive for the enslaved Africans brought to America not to pray.

For the most part, the white masters wanted their slaves to grab hold of the Christian faith. Their thinking behind this was that Christianity would make the slaves more docile. Yet and still, these masters were not prepared for their slaves to bring their tears, anguish, and heartache before the Living God in prayer and supplication. They certainly weren't prepared for the Living God to answer.

Something happens during prayer. God's government which is a very different government from our own earthly systems, enters into the material realm and begins the process of over throwing the establish kingdoms of this world. I am certain that African Americans have their freedom today because these men and women, our forerunners of the faith, pressed through and prayed. Prayer, the kind of prayer I'm going to be talking about in this book, *Intercession the Heart Beat of God* is a revolutionary act.

As part of our study together I'm going to encourage you to read the scriptures out loud. The Word of God tells us in Romans 10:17 that faith comes by hearing the Word of God. I believe that with all my might. I believe that another level of faith comes to us when we hear the Word of God spoken over our lives. In each chapter of this book, I will give you a principle so by the time we are done you will have nine principles as it relates to prayer that you can hang your hat on so to speak. The first principle is this:

## PRINCIPLE #1
### PRAYER IS A REVOLUTIONARY ACT.

## Matthew 16: 13-20

*[13] When Jesus came to the region of Caesarea Philippi, he asked his disciples, "Who do people say the Son of Man is?"[14] They replied, "Some say John the Baptist; others say Elijah; and still others, Jeremiah or one of the prophets."[15] "But what about you?" he asked. "Who do you say I am?"[16] Simon Peter answered, "You are the Messiah, the Son of the living God."[17] Jesus replied, "Blessed are you, Simon son of Jonah, for this was not revealed to you by flesh and blood, but by my Father in heaven. [18] And I tell you that you are Peter,[a] and on this rock I will build my church, and the gates of Hades will not overcome it. [19] I will give you the keys of the kingdom of heaven; whatever you bind on earth will be bound in heaven, and whatever you loose on earth will be loosed in heaven."[20] Then he ordered his disciples not to tell anyone that he was the Messiah.*

The above passage talks about the formation of the modern-day church. There is a lot of chatter in the earth realm about who Jesus is and Jesus knows it. So He asks His disciples, "Who do men say I am?" They tell Him all the rumors and then Jesus asks them another question, "But what about you, who do you say I am?" Peter is the first one to catch hold of the revelation and replies, "You are the Son of God." Peter is the author of many firsts. He was the first person to get out of the boat when he saw Jesus walking on the water. He was the first person to really catch the revelation about who Jesus really is. He was the first person to fight on Jesus's behalf. You may remember that Peter chopped off the guard's ear when they came to apprehend Jesus. Jesus wasn't too happy about that, but, all things considered, Jesus likes Peter's spirit.

So Jesus makes an apostolic mandate. He says, "Blessed are you Peter, because flesh and blood didn't reveal this to you. This came to you from God. Your name means Rock and I'm going to build my church upon you." And from this moment forward, Peter becomes The Church. This is important to note, because every word that Jesus speaks to Peter from henceforth, applies to the whole church. Jesus tells Peter that the gates of Hell won't be able to prevail against him—the church, not Peter, per se. But the Church, the edifice that Jesus would build upon Peter. Please understand, if the foundation that Jesus is building upon is a man, then we can rest assured that the stones are also made up of living breathing believers.

There are two very important points I want you to remember concerning this passage. Number one: Jesus is telling us the method by which His church would receive revelation. He says people are going to be throwing out educated guesses, or offering up scientific explanations, but His church would receive their insight and understanding directly from God.

This is a very big deal given the time period. Today, we as believers, have the Holy Spirit living on the inside of us. God can speak to our hearts at any time He chooses, but Jesus is speaking during a time period we refer to as, pre-Holy Ghost dispensation.

In fact, there were times in Israel's history that God went completely silent. In the book of Malachi, the last book of the Old Testament. God says to His people, "Stop, stop! Hold the presses! I don't want your tithe anymore. You're bringing me lame goats and blind sheep that you found on the way to church. Your heart isn't in this. Your worship is just for show. So let's just forget about it, okay?" Heaven is completely silent for 400 years and the next voice we hear is John's. The voice crying out in the wilderness, "Prepare the way for the Lord." So for Peter, an unlearned fishermen, who does not come from a priestly or prophetic lineage, to actually receive revelation from God— it's a really, really, big deal. In fact, I'd say that it was revolutionary. Just as in the days before Samuel came to live in the temple, the Word of God was very rare in Peter's day.

The next take away I want you to receive from this passage is that Jesus is telling us, His church, that we will have power to affect supernatural change in both the Heaven and the Earth. This is also revolutionary and an exceedingly great gift. Heretofore, Israel had only ever known of two people in the history of the planet to walk in the type of supernatural power that Jesus was now purporting that all believers would be able to have— Moses and Elijah.

Let's read the next two passage together:

## Genesis 18:1-8, 16-33

*The LORD appeared to Abraham near the great trees of Mamre while he was sitting at the entrance to his tent in the heat of the day. ² Abraham looked up and saw three men standing nearby. When he saw them, he hurried from the entrance of his tent to meet them and bowed low to the ground.³ He said, "If I have found favor in your eyes, my lord do not pass your servant by. ⁴ Let a little water be brought, and then you may all wash your feet and rest under this tree. ⁵ Let me get you something to eat, so you can be refreshed and then go on your way—now that you have come to your servant." "Very well," they answered, "do as you say."⁶ So Abraham hurried into the tent to Sarah. "Quick," he said, "get three seahs of the finest flour and knead it and bake some bread."⁷ Then he ran to the herd and selected a choice, tender calf and gave it to a servant, who hurried to prepare it. ⁸ He then brought some curds and milk and the calf that had been prepared, and set these before them. While they ate, he stood near them under a tree.*

*[16] When the men got up to leave, they looked down toward Sodom, and Abraham walked along with them to see them on their way. [17] Then the LORD said, "Shall I hide from Abraham what I am about to do? [18] Abraham will surely become a great and powerful nation, and all nations on earth will be blessed through him. [19] For I have chosen him, so that he will direct his children and his household after him to keep the way of the LORD by doing what is right and just, so that the LORD will bring about for Abraham what he has promised him." [20] Then the LORD said, "The outcry against Sodom and Gomorrah is so great and their sin so grievous [21] that I will go down and see if what they have done is as bad as the outcry that has reached me. If not, I will know." [22] The men turned away and went toward Sodom, but Abraham remained standing before the LORD. [23] Then Abraham approached him and said: "Will you sweep away the righteous with the wicked? [24] What if there are fifty righteous people in the city? Will you really sweep it away and not spare the place for the sake of the fifty righteous people in it? [25] Far be it from you to do such a thing—to kill the righteous with the wicked, treating the righteous and the wicked alike. Far be it from you! Will not the Judge of all the earth do right?" [26] The LORD said, "If I find fifty righteous people in the city of Sodom, I will spare the whole place for their sake." [27] Then Abraham spoke up again: "Now that I have been so bold as to speak to*

*the Lord, though I am nothing but dust and ashes, $^{28}$ what if the number of the righteous is five less than fifty? Will you destroy the whole city for lack of five people?"*

*"If I find forty-five there," he said, "I will not destroy it."$^{29}$ Once again he spoke to him, "What if only forty are found there? "He said, "For the sake of forty, I will not do it."$^{30}$ Then he said, "May the Lord not be angry, but let me speak. What if only thirty can be found there? "He answered, "I will not do it if I find thirty there."$^{31}$ Abraham said, "Now that I have been so bold as to speak to the Lord, what if only twenty can be found there?" He said, "For the sake of twenty, I will not destroy it."$^{32}$ Then he said, "May the Lord not be angry, but let me speak just once more. What if only ten can be found there?" He answered, "For the sake of ten, I will not destroy it."$^{33}$ When the LORD had finished speaking with Abraham, he left, and Abraham returned home.*

I've included this particular story in scripture because I want you to see that everything about this passage is remarkably revolutionary. Abraham is cooling out, sitting outside his tent. He sees the Lord appear in human form and he recognizes Him right away. This is not the Trinity. It is the Lord with two angelic escorts. We know it's not the Father because scripture tells us that no man has seen the Father and lived. This is a picture of the Pre-incarnate Christ who comes to visit Abraham. And Abraham recognizes Him right off. Abraham runs to Him, bows low to the ground and greets the Lord. This is

Jesus, the Commander of the Lord's Army, coming into the earth realm to inspect the situation currently going on in Sodom and Gomorrah.

According to scripture, God had been hearing some complaints. We know that in Genesis 4:10, Abel's blood cried out from the earth. Romans 8:19-22 tells us that the earth groans. So we don't know where these complaints are coming from, people, blood, or the earth. We just know that the complaints have reached Heaven and that they are so bad that God has come to check it out for Himself. The Lord decides to do something remarkable. He stops and has a meal with Abraham. There is no other place mentioned in the Bible where the Pre-incarnate Christ sits down for a meal with anyone. Plenty of people offer him food but for everyone else God just turns their offering into a burnt sacrifice. But with Abraham, God sits and sups. Then, God decides that based on the territorial holding that He Himself has bequeathed to Abraham, that Abraham had the right to be informed about the Sodom and Gomorrah situation. Abraham hears God's plan and he decides to intervene.

You might want to take a minute to find a highlighter if you don't already have one. Highlight that sentence and read it again. **Abraham decides to intervene.** Oftentimes we see things going on in our world and we just go about our business because we don't feel the unction to pray. Abraham didn't wait for an unction he decided to intervene. But what I really want you to see is that God had already tested him and found that Abraham had the type of sensitivity that God was looking for. God is walking by— passing through the earth realm in human form and out of all the people on the earth at that time, Abraham had the sensitivity to discern who He is. How many people let the Saviour pass them by that day? I want you to know something, Beloved, every single one of us is called to the ministry of intercession but not everyone of us will answer that call.

This same man, Abraham, who had the sensitivity to recognize God walking by in human form also had the foresight, wisdom, and sensitivity to know that right there—in that moment, the Creator wanted Him to intervene. So now we have a situation where one ruler is talking to another ruler. The two of them enter into negotiations about a matter happening in the earth. Don't forget Lot lives in the area in question, so this isn't just about Abraham's physical holdings. It's also about his family connections. Lot is a part of Abraham's spiritual territory. Abraham is literally in the gap before the Lord on behalf of the land. The two of them, God and Abraham speak as governing authorities. Not equals. Abraham understands that, that's why during these negotiations he refers to himself as dust. But God has elevated him in this moment to stand before him and do business on behalf of two major cities at that time in the earth.

I want you to understand that when the Lord went walking by Abraham's tent that day, He wasn't looking for Abraham. He was looking for agreement from an intercessor. He was looking for someone to stand in the gap on behalf of the land so that He would not have to destroy it. He found Abraham. As I read this passage, I can't help but feel that the Lord is very pleased and proud of Abraham for having the courage to enter into these negotiations with Him. Abraham is behaving in exactly the way that God wants. This is the kind of intercession that God expects. Let's read the next passage together:

## Exodus 32:7-14

*Then the LORD said to Moses, "Go down, because your people, whom you brought up out of Egypt, have become corrupt. ⁸ They have been quick to turn away from what I commanded them and have made themselves an idol cast in the shape of a calf. They have bowed down to it and sacrificed to it and have said, 'These are your gods, Israel, who brought you up out of Egypt.' ⁹ "I have seen these people," the LORD said to Moses, "and they are a stiff-necked people. ¹⁰ Now leave me alone so that my anger may burn against them and that I may destroy them. Then I will make you into a great nation."*

*¹¹ But Moses sought the favor of the LORD his God. "LORD," he said, "why should your anger burn against your people, whom you brought out of Egypt with great power and a mighty hand? ¹² Why should the Egyptians say, 'It was with evil intent that he brought them out, to kill them in the mountains and to wipe them off the face of the earth'? Turn from your fierce anger; relent and do not bring disaster on your people. [13] Remember your servants Abraham, Isaac and Israel, to whom you swore by your own self: I will make your descendants as numerous as the stars in the sky and I will give your descendants all this land I promised them, and it will be their inheritance forever.'" [14] Then the LORD relented and did not bring on his people the disaster he had threatened.*

We all know Moses, right? Moses is the only person documented in the history of the world to have seen God's backside. Moses was minding his own business in the desert, tending his father-in law's flock when the Lord came to visit him. God said, "Hey, I got a job for you to do. The Israelites have been in slavery for the last 400 years, their cries have reached up to Heaven and caused me to remember my covenant with the great patriarch, Abraham. I've decided to raise up a deliverer and that deliverer is you, Moses. So, go set my people free."

By the time the particular incident in Exodus 32 happened, Moses had totally bought into the plan of God. He had totally changed the whole trajectory of his life. He's been in the presence of God 24 hours a day for the last 40 days, receiving dictation from Heaven. Moses and God are up on the mountaintop writing the first five books of the Bible and the people are down in the valley sinning.

God says. "Moses, you've got a problem. The people you brought out from Egypt are down there sinning.

Now leave me alone so that my anger can burn against them." Moses says, "Wait, time out, God, these aren't my people, these are your people." This is probably the most crucial passage in Jewish history. The whole Nation is hanging in the balance, in the hands of Moses, one intercessor and God's mind is made up. God has decided to put these people to death. We know His mind is made up because He's looking for other ways to fulfill His covenant to Abraham. God offers Moses are really, really sweet deal. He says. "I'll tell you what. How about I destroy them and make you into a mighty nation. Moses, you're a descendant of Abraham, this can still work." Moses is the perfect person for this job. He's jealous for God's name and yet he has an awesome love for the people he is standing in the gap for. Moses says, "Please God, don't kill them. If you kill them, all your enemies are going to say it's because you didn't have the power to deliver them in the first place."

Here's the thing I want you to see. I want you to see what God is really doing when He tells Moses that these are, "your people." He isn't so angry that He has momentary taken leave of His senses. On the contrary, it's quite the opposite. In His anger, God is providing a way of escape for His people through the vehicle of the deliverer called Moses. When God calls Israel, "Moses's people" He is informing Moses of his territorial rights. "The moment you brought them up out of bondage, they became your territory, Moses. These are your people."

This is vitally important, because now it means that Moses can intervene. He can enter into negotiations with God on behalf of the Israelites. Just as his predecessor Abraham did on behalf of Sodom and Gomorrah.

There is another reason that Moses's intercession is vitally required in this moment. God is not moved right now because of His own relationship with the people. Moses tries to reason with God by reminding Him of that. "God they are your people." God's not moved by that. God is looking for a way to exact judgment on the people and still keep His Word to Abraham. What does matter to God, however, in this moment, is Moses's agreement. Moses doesn't pray his own will. His heart is totally in alignment with the plan of God. Therefore, he reminds God of His Word. This is Romans 8:26-27 in action even though technically in this juncture in history, it hasn't been written yet. This is the Spirit of God praying through Moses the heart of God.

Have you ever prayed a prayer that blew your own mind? You were amazed at the words that were coming out of your mouth? This is exactly what happened to Moses and what happened to Abraham in the previous passage. These mere mortals cannot believe that they are doing business with God like this. This is the same God that would have to hide Moses in the cleft of a rock while He passed by him so that His glory wouldn't accidentally kill him. It's the same God that when his celestial messengers appear to deliver a message to people, the glory that surrounds the angels, just from being in God's presence, is so great, that they have to strengthen mortals to keep them from passing out before they can deliver the message. Yet these two men are negotiating with the Maker of Heaven and Earth, each one doing business with the Living God.

If you don't remember anything else from this chapter, I want you to remember that prayer is a revolutionary act. If you rise up and answer the call to intercession, you will become a revolutionary too.

†

# CHAPTER TWO
# STANDING IN THE GAP

In this chapter we are going to be looking at what it really means to stand in the gap. These four little words, "standing in the gap" have become a churchy catchphrase. A lot of folks in churchdom are talking about it, but most people don't really know how to do it. Together, as we study the scriptures, I believe that you will gain a fuller revelation about what it means to stand in the gap on behalf of the land. My prayer is that as you read this section, your understanding will increase, and that your newfound understanding will propel you into the gap on behalf of others.

## Ephesians 4:11-13

*[11] So Christ himself gave the apostles, the prophets, the evangelists, the pastors and teachers, [12] to equip his people for works of service, so that the body of Christ may be built up [13] until we all reach unity in the faith and in the knowledge of the Son of God and become mature, attaining to the whole measure of the fullness of Christ.*

I want you to pay attention to the word built in the above passage, because you will see it several times during the course of our study. I also want you to notice that in this passage there is no specific call to the office of intercession listed here or anywhere else in the scriptures. Yet and still, we recognize the ministry of intercession as a vital gift to the body of Christ. So, the question we are left to ponder is this: who in the world is supposed to pray? I won't leave you in suspense. I don't really like to be left in suspense myself, so I'll just go ahead and tell you. Apostles are called to pray. Prophets are called to pray. Evangelists are called to pray. Pastors are called to pray. Teachers are called to pray. Deacons are called to pray. Ushers are called to pray. Children are called to pray. Cute people, fat people, old people, poor people, and you can fill in the blank with whomever else you want because if you are breathing, if you have a pulse, if you are a spirit man enclosed inside a dirt body and you live on the planet Earth, you are called to pray. Let's take a look at the next two passages together, Isaiah 59:15-16, and Ezekiel 22:30-31.

## Isaiah 59:15-16

*Truth is nowhere to be found, and whoever shuns evil becomes a prey. The LORD looked and was displeased that there was no justice. $^{16}$ He saw that there was no one, he was appalled that there was no one to intervene; so his own arm achieved salvation for him, and his own righteousness sustained him.*

## Ezekiel 22:30-31

*³⁰ "I looked for someone among them who would build up the wall and stand before me in the gap on behalf of the land so I would not have to destroy it, but I found no one. ³¹ So I will pour out my wrath on them and consume them with my fiery anger, bringing down on their own heads all they have done, declares the Sovereign LORD."*

According to Isaiah 59, and Ezekiel 22, God has two expectations. The first expectation is that someone would build up the wall. The second expectation is that someone would stand before Him in the gap on behalf of the land so that He won't have to destroy it. We often group these two operations together but building up the wall and standing in the gap are two separate functions of intercession. The Isaiah 59 and the Ezekiel 22 passages both also relay to us God's feelings on injustice. We learn that He is displeased with injustice. Other words for displeased would be annoyed, irritated, or peeved. However, we learn that God is appalled by the fact that there was no one there to intercede. Other words for appalled would be shocked, horrified or disgusted. So based on our study of both the Isaiah 59 passage and Ezekiel 22 passage, we can conclude that God hates prayerlessness even more than He hates injustice.

Listen Beloved, God's court is the highest court in the land. If we are not coming before His court petitioning Him for the Earth, then injustice will flourish. Pay attention anywhere in the Word of God, where God says something more than once. If God repeats Himself that means, it's pretty important to Him. It also means we didn't quite catch the fullness the first time He said it. Anytime God repeats Himself in the Holy Scriptures He's telling us that there is a deeper meaning behind the text. Therefore, we, the readers, should pay closer attention. The next passage I want us to read together is Matthew 18.

## Matthew 18:15-20:

*"If your brother or sister sins go and point out their fault, just between the two of you. If they listen to you, you have won them over. But if they will not listen, take one or two others along, so that 'every matter may be established by the testimony of two or three witnesses. If they still refuse to listen, tell it to the church; and if they refuse to listen even to the church, treat them as you would a pagan or a tax collector. "Truly, I tell you, whatever you bind on earth will be bound in heaven, and whatever you loose on earth will be loosed in heaven. "Again, truly I tell you that if two of you on earth agree about anything they ask for, it will be done for them by my Father in heaven. [20] For where two or three gather in my name, there am I with them."*

This passage is closely related to the Matthew 16 passage we read in the first chapter of this book. They are similar in that they both talk about binding and loosing. Even still, you can't just read one passage and not the other because they each contain information that the other passage doesn't have. For example, in addition to binding and loosing, Matthew 18 tells us how we are to deal with sin in the church. Jesus says first try and handle it yourself. When or if that doesn't work, then take along one or two other believers. If that doesn't work, then you take the person operating in sin before the church. The statement directly after that is, if two of you on earth agree about anything it will be done by my Father. This statement lets you know what this passage is really about. In other words, this passage is about intercession but it's not necessarily about prayer. You see beloved, there is a whole lot of things that should happen in the gap. Let's read 1 John 5:16 for a little more insight.

## 1 John 5:16

*<sup>16</sup> If you see any brother or sister commit a sin that does not lead to death, you should pray and God will give them life. I refer to those whose sin does not lead to death. There is a sin that leads to death. I am not saying that you should pray about that.*

I really like this particular passage in 1 John because it tells us **how** we are to operate in the gap. Sometimes you see something that is off or awry in your sister or brother in Christ's life and the solution is to pray about it quietly and God will set things right. But if you see your brethren doing something that will lead to their demise you don't get in the gap and pray. You get in the gap and you confront and wrestle.

Now in order for this to work, relationship is essential. You can't be in the gap for someone unless you have relationship with one or more of the parties involved in the dispute. That's the nature of mediation. In other words, if you don't talk to God on a regular basis, you probably aren't going to be a very effective intercessor for me when Heaven makes a claim against me. Now that being said, the reverse of this is also true. Maybe you don't talk to Heaven often, but you have relationship with the one you are praying for. The greatest intercessors are those who are moved by their relationship for the people whom they are praying for.

Now let me be clear and say that the 1 John 5:16 passage is not about a brother or sister wronging you. It's about standing in between sin and your brother or sister. This passage is talking about something in your brother or sister's life that impedes their relationship with Christ. The scripture tells us that you should become the intermediary between Christ and them. Scripture says first try talking to them, see if you can pull them away from the sin. If you can't pull them apart, then take along one or two more believers.

Standing in the gap requires us to get up close and personal. Sometimes it means squeezing or interjecting oneself into a tight place. Sometimes that may mean asking uncomfortable questions or getting intimately involved in the details of someone's sorted mess. We see things happening every day that are clearly wrong, but we don't act as a go-between because we tell ourselves, "That's not really my business. Or who am I to judge?" Doing business for and with God means you make it your business. Being an intercessor for God says you get all up in between the person and their sin. That's what it means to intercede. If the person won't listen, scripture says take along a few other people, see if you can't widen the gap between your brother or sister and the thing that's impeding them. If that won't work, then let the whole church jump in the gap and intercede. And if that won't work, human will is surely involved, and there isn't a thing you can do with somebody's will. Scripture says to treat them like an unbeliever. But the very next statement after that is: truly if two of you on earth agree about ANYTHING it will be done by my Father in Heaven. This tells me that no matter what the initial outcome is, prayer will always work. Even if they walk away from righteousness altogether, you can put a demand on that person's life. This scripture verse assures us that it is possible to snatch anybody, anywhere out of the jaws of death. Now, let's read 1Samuel 16 together and take a look at some other ways of standing in the gap.

## 1 Samuel 16: 14-23

*Now the Spirit of the Lord had departed from Saul, and an evil spirit from the Lord tormented him.15Saul's attendants said to him, "See, an evil spirit from God is tormenting you. 16Let our lord command his servants here to search for someone who can play the lyre. He will play when the evil spirit from God comes on you, and you will feel better." 17So Saul said to his attendants, "Find someone who plays well and bring him to me." 18One of the servants answered, "I have seen a son of Jesse of Bethlehem who knows how to play the lyre. He is a brave man and a warrior. He speaks well and is a fine-looking man. And the Lord is with him." 19Then Saul sent messengers to Jesse and said, "Send me your son David, who is with the sheep." 20So Jesse took a donkey loaded with bread, a skin of wine and a young goat and sent them with his son David to Saul. 21David came to Saul and entered his service. Saul liked him very much, and David became one of his armor-bearers. 22Then Saul sent word to Jesse, saying, "Allow David to remain in my service, for I am pleased with him. 23Whenever the spirit from God came on Saul, David would take up his lyre and play. Then relief would come to Saul; he would feel better, and the evil spirit would leave him.*

I just want to start off by saying it's a miracle before God that David ever even became King. This is a rags to riches tale if I've ever heard one. God promised David the kingdom when he was lowly and despised, just a steward over a few sheep. David's family was not rich. They didn't have cattle, scripture says they had a few sheep. But here is the thing I want you to see. God brings David into the palace into the service of the king as an intercessor. Some of you reading this right now, God has promised you some things that are just mind-blowingly miraculous. You have no idea how those things that God has whispered to your heart are going to come to pass.

Some of you are waiting on God to do what He said, and God is waiting on the type of intercession to come out of your mouth that will shift atmospheres, and governments. The kind of intercession that will bring you to the palace.

David's intercession, his worship, in particular, had the ability to shift governments. Please understand that at this point in David's career, David had never even picked up a sword. He had not yet killed Goliath. Yet he was known throughout the land as a brave man, and a warrior. He was just a shepherd tending his father's flock. But if a lion or a bear tried to run off with one of his sheep the Spirit of the Lord would come upon David and David would kill the lion and the bear.

Now if we were to read this passage in the King James Version it would tell us that David was "cunning" on the harp. If we were to look up that word "cunning" we'd find the word "skill". Yet the word cunning seems to denote something more than skill. David had a particular set of skills. There was a supernatural element to David's musical abilities. Let us not forget that the evil spirit that tormented Saul was sent by God. Yet, even still, when David began to play the harp he had the supernatural ability to touch God's heart and to change God's mind. David is worshipping in the gap.

# Joel 2: 17

*Let the priests, the ministers of the LORD, weep between the porch and the altar, and let them say, Spare your people, O LORD, and give not your heritage to reproach, that the heathen should rule over them: why should they say among the people, Where is their God?*

This porch and altar language in Joel chapter two refers to the layout of the ancient Temple. The porch was located in the front of the sanctuary. Beyond the porch was the entrance into the Holy Place. The porch opened into the Inner Court which contained the large altar. This place between the porch and altar was the place where the priests made intercession on behalf of the people of God who remained in the outer court, just beyond the walls.

What's interesting to me about the book of Joel is that biblical scholars have a very hard time dating it. No one can say with certainty whether Joel was written before the exile or afterward. No one can say this because the writer doesn't mention a king or any other useful information to help historians orientate the book in history. In a very real sense this makes the book of Joel timeless.

I believe the Lord had Joel to purposely leave out historical references, so that the people of God wouldn't make the mistake of thinking that this particular passage doesn't apply to us all. Because the truth is, it doesn't matter what century you live in, or what generation or age, the priest of God will always need to weep and cry out for the people of God. Our hearts must break for what breaks God's heart. Anyone who has spent any time in ministry and seen the brokenness in both leaders and laymen know this. There is a whole lot of mess going on between the porch and the altar. The ministers of God need to raise up a lament. Which brings me to my next principle:

# PRINCIPLE # 2

**SOMETIMES YOU MUST WEEP IN THE GAP. SOMETIMES YOU MUST WORSHIP IN THE GAP. SOMETIMES YOU MUST WRESTLE & CONFRONT PEOPLE OR SPIRTUAL FORCES OF WICKEDNESS IN THE GAP.**

✝

# CHAPTER THREE
# REPAIRING THE BREACHES

Intercessors get news, especially bad news. Information just always seems to find you when you're an intercessor, some way or another you stumble upon it. Of course, what you do with that news will determine whether you are a gossip or an intercessor.

In the Nehemiah passage we are about to read below, you will see that Nehemiah is just a regular guy with a good city job. He was not in the ministry. He's an ordinary person. He hears some troubling news from back home and he makes the decision to raise up a lament before the Lord.

As you read, I want you to consciously take a moment and pull apart his prayer. Because when you do, you'll see that number one, he fully understands why his people went into captivity and number two, he understands what needs to occur for them to get out. Nehemiah understands that somebody needs to repent.

Please note that this passage doesn't say that the whole nation repented. It doesn't even say that Nehemiah called some concerned citizens together and they had a prayer meeting. This passage says that one man stood in the gap and repented on behalf of the nation and God heard his plea.

## Nehemiah 1: 1-11

*1The words of Nehemiah son of Hakaliah: In the month of Kislev in the twentieth year, while I was in the citadel of Susa, 2Hanani, one of my brothers, came from Judah with some other men, and I questioned them about the Jewish remnant that had survived the exile, and also about Jerusalem.3They said to me, "Those who survived the exile and are back in the province are in great trouble and disgrace. The wall of Jerusalem is broken down, and its gates have been burned with fire."4When I heard these things, I sat down and wept. For some days I mourned and fasted and prayed before the God of heaven. 5Then I said: "Lord, the God of heaven, the great and awesome God, who keeps his covenant of love with those who love him and keep his commandments, 6 let your ear be attentive and your eyes open to hear the prayer your servant is praying before you day and night for your servants, the people of Israel. I confess the sins we Israelites, including myself and my father's family, have committed against you. 7We have acted very wickedly toward you. We have not obeyed the commands, decrees and laws you gave your servant Moses.8"Remember the instruction you gave your servant Moses, saying, 'If you are unfaithful, I will scatter you among the nations, 9but if you return to me and obey my commands, then even if your exiled people are at the farthest horizon, I will gather them from there and bring them to the place I have chosen as a dwelling for my Name.' 10 "They are your servants and your people, whom you redeemed by your great strength and your mighty hand. 11Lord, let your ear be attentive to the prayer of this your servant and to the prayer of your servants who delight in revering your name. Give your servant success today by granting him favor in the presence of this man." I was cupbearer to the king.*

If you've had the pleasure of reading the whole book of Nehemiah, which I hope you have, you can see that Nehemiah is a man of precise vision who was able to rebuild the wall that surrounded the entire city in an amazing fifty-two-day campaign. What I want you to see from the passage above, is that Nehemiah is a skillful intercessor. He understands both the One he is praying to and the people he is interceding for. He has familiarized himself with God's Word and he also has historical data about the people he is standing in the gap for. It is while Nehemiah is in the gap that he begins to repair the breach.

Webster's defines "breach" this way:

1. A failure to do what is required by a law and agreement or duty: failure to act in a required or promised way.
2. A break in friendly relations between people or groups.

3. A hole or opening in something (such as a wall) made by breaking through it.

Sin represents not only a failure to live out God's law. Sin creates holes in our walls. It is through these holes or breaches that our enemies both spiritually and naturally can enter in and take us into captivity. Nehemiah cries out to the Living God. He knows the reason why his people went into captivity in the first place: because they didn't honor God or keep His commandments. Nehemiah confesses his sin, his father's family sins, and his nation's sins. He says, "God, I remember your word that says if we are unfaithful you would scatter us among the nations, now God please remember what you said you would do once we repented and obeyed you. You would gather us up again and bring us into a place where your name can be honored." And even though this is exactly what Nehemiah wants God to do, for the sake of his countrymen, Nehemiah is absolutely praying God's will because he is also praying God's word.

Let's take a look for a moment at our next two passages of study.

## Leviticus 26:40-42

*'But if they will confess their sins and the sins of their ancestors—their unfaithfulness and their hostility toward me, 41which made me hostile toward them so that I sent them into the land of their enemies—then*

*when their uncircumcised hearts are humbled and they pay for their sin, 42 I will remember my covenant with Jacob and my covenant with Isaac and my covenant with Abraham, and I will remember the land.*

## 2 Chronicles 7:14

*If my people, who are called by my name, will humble themselves and pray and seek my face and turn from their wicked ways, then I will hear from heaven, and I will forgive their sin and will heal their land.*

In these two passages we see what it means to repair the breaches in the wall. To confess personal sin, and corporate sin on behalf of the family, or nation or an institution you are praying for. God requires us to humble, seek, and turn, before He will hear. The end result of this type of intercession is that healing will come to the land. Many times, the people of God are unsuccessful in prayer because we don't first go up in the spirit and repair the holes or breaches in the wall that are left there as a result of sin.

## Ezekiel 13:1-5

*The word of the LORD came to me: ² "Son of man, prophesy against the prophets of Israel who are now prophesying. Say to those who prophesy out of their own imagination: 'Hear the word of the LORD! ³ This* *is what the Sovereign LORD says: Woe to the foolish prophets who follow their own spirit and have seen nothing! $^4$ Your prophets, Israel, are like jackals among ruins. $^5$ You have not gone up to the breaches in the wall to repair it for the people of Israel so that it will stand firm in the battle on the day of the LORD.*

Please note that we will be discussing more about the role of the prophet during intercession a little later on in this study, but for now, I want to use this passage and the following passage in Ezekiel 13 as **an example of some things that prophets should not do.**

## Ezekiel 13: 10-13

*10 "'Because they lead my people astray, saying, "Peace," when there is no peace, and because, when a flimsy wall is built, they cover it with whitewash, 11 therefore tell those who cover it with whitewash that it is going to fall. Rain will come in torrents, and I will send hailstones hurtling down, and violent winds will burst forth. 12 When the wall collapses, will people not ask you, "Where is the whitewash you covered it with?" 13 "'Therefore this is what the Sovereign LORD says: In my wrath I will unleash a violent wind, and in my anger hailstones and torrents of rain will fall with destructive fury. 14 I will tear down the wall you have covered with whitewash and will level it to the ground so that its foundation will be laid bare. When it falls, you will be destroyed in it; and you will know that I am the LORD*

One of the most important duties of the prophet, is to prepare the house of God for the day of judgment—to "see" the breaks in the walls—the areas where His church is weak, those places where the enemy can slip in unaware, and repair them. God rebuked the foolish prophets of Ezekiel's day because they had not "gone up" to the breaks in the wall to "repair it…"

History tells us that the walls that fortified cities in biblical days where several thousands of feet high, and wide. God didn't intend for His prophets to scale the walls with a can of spackle in their hands and repair the holes—but He did intend for them to engage in a level of spiritual warfare whereby they had to "go up" in the spiritual realm and deal with the problems going on in their cities.

Ezekiel 13:10-13, is specifically talking about the foolish prophets who prophesy out of their own imagination. When the people of God built flimsy walls of protection, the prophets came right behind them and put whitewash on the walls. In other words, the prophets put their agreement on things that would not last.

So how do you build a flimsy wall? You build a flimsy wall when you try to build a foundation of prayer without starting with repentance. You build a flimsy wall when the prophets and the intercessors pay no attention to the true condition of the houses of worship they have been called to guard. When the prophets and intercessors turn a blind eye to what is actually going on in a house because they love, respect or even idolize the leadership and or the people. When the prophets cry peace when God isn't saying peace. When prophets began to prophesy out of the soulish realm instead of the spirit realm, a flimsy wall is being built. It is actually quite easy to begin to slip into prophesying what people want to hear instead of what the Spirit of the Lord is saying. There are many competing voices in the spirit realm and all it takes is for the vessel to be one millimeter off. That's how the prophetic people of God begin to whitewash the walls. That's why we have to 'go up' to the high places in order to correctly build the wall.

When we go up past this temporal realm, past our own understanding, we begin to see like God sees. As humans we often trick ourselves into thinking we know the mind of God or that we understand His heart. Yet the scriptures tell us clearly that our ways are not His ways, neither are our thoughts His thoughts. We have to climb past this realm, press past the second realm, press ourselves into the glory realm in order to obtain His thoughts. We are going to be talking more about what this type of pressing prayer looks like in chapter four, but for now, the final thought I want to leave you with in this chapter is the $3^{rd}$ principle.

# PRINCIPLE #3

**ONE OF THE ESSENTIAL DUTIES OF GOD'S END TIME PROPHETS IS TO SOUND THE ALARM & CALL THE PEOPLE OF GOD BACK TO PRAYERFULNESS. TO GO UP IN THE SPIRIT REALM, AND REPAIR THE BREACHES.**

# INTERCESSION
# The Heart Beat of God

## Part II
## The Press
## Backlash & Retaliation
## Avengers & Redeemers

✝

# CHAPTER FOUR
# THE PRESS

What's pressing prayer? It's intense prayer. It's the type of prayer that overcomes your flesh. It's uncomfortable. If this was the 4$^{th}$ Watch and you were praying with me and the other intercessors on our team, I would tell you, "If you aren't sweating yet, then you aren't pressing yet." When you press you pray in such a way as if to say, "Heaven will hear me today!"

You might be saying to yourself, "God is a God of Love. He wants us to come to Him in prayer so why do I have to go through all of this 'pressing business' just to have an encounter with Him?" The answer is a rather simple truth. God wants you to have an encounter with Him but the enemy of our souls doesn't want that encounter to occur. If you've read my book, *Doing Business with God,* you'll know my perspective on prayer. Prayer is a conversation with God. It is the divine privilege and birthright of every person on the planet (not just Christians) to have this interaction with The Creator. However, the moment you try and claim this divine privilege, the moment you decide to seize your destiny, to grab ahold of Christ for the very thing which He grabbed a hold of you for—communion and relationship with Him, you declare war on the demonic kingdom. Yes, little ole you, standing inside your purpose, walking in your destiny is a personal affront to the devil. Who would have thunk it, huh? I am convinced more than ever that you cannot birth your destiny without a press.

In this chapter we are going to be reading a lot of scripture verses back to back. Every one of them being relevant to understanding this oftentimes elusive and metaphorical concept of the press. I'm not going to offer any explanation in between the passages as I have in previous chapters because I want the Word of God to settle in your spirit. I want it to ignite you. I want it to create a churning inside of you. I want the spirit of, Heaven- will- hear- me- today to come alive inside you. Let's begin.

## Genesis 32:22-32

*$^{22}$ That night Jacob got up and took his two wives, his two female servants and his eleven sons and crossed the ford of the Jabbok. $^{23}$ After he had sent them across the stream, he sent over all his possessions. $^{24}$ So Jacob was left alone, and a man wrestled with him till daybreak. $^{25}$ When the man saw that he could not overpower him, he touched the socket of Jacob's hip so that his hip was wrenched as he wrestled with the man. $^{26}$ Then the man said, "Let me go, for it is daybreak." But Jacob replied, "I will not let you go unless you bless me."$^{27}$ The man asked him, "What is your name?" "Jacob," he answered.$^{28}$ Then the man*

*said, "Your name will no longer be Jacob, but Israel, because you have struggled with God and with humans and have overcome."*

## Luke 8:43-48

*$^{43}$ And a woman was there who had been subject to bleeding for twelve years, but no one could heal her. $^{44}$ She came up behind him and touched the edge of his cloak, and immediately her bleeding stopped. $^{45}$ "Who touched me?" Jesus asked. When they all denied it, Peter said, "Master, the people are crowding and pressing against you."$^{46}$ But Jesus said, "Someone touched me; I know that power has gone out from me."$^{47}$ Then the woman, seeing that she could not go unnoticed, came trembling and fell at his feet. In the presence of all the people, she told why she had touched him and how she had been instantly healed. $^{48}$ Then he said to her, "Daughter, your faith has healed you. Go in peace."*

## Hebrews 5:7

*During the days of Jesus' life on earth, he offered up prayers and petitions with fervent cries and tears to the one who could save him from death, and he was heard because of his reverent submission.*

## Luke 18 1-8

*Then Jesus told his disciples a parable to show them that they should always pray and not give up. ² He said: "In a certain town there was a judge who neither feared God nor cared what people thought. ³ And there was a widow in that town who kept coming to him with the plea, 'Grant me justice against my adversary.' ⁴ "For some time he refused. But finally he said to himself, 'Even though I don't fear God or care what people think, ⁵ yet because this widow keeps bothering me, I will see that she gets justice, so that she won't eventually come and attack me!'" ⁶ And the Lord said, "Listen to what the unjust judge says. ⁷ And will not God bring about justice for his chosen ones, who cry out to him day and night? Will he keep putting them off? ⁸ I tell you, he will see that they get justice, and quickly. However, when the Son of Man comes, will he find faith on the earth?"*

## Acts 19: 11-16

*God did extraordinary miracles through Paul, ¹² so that even handkerchiefs and aprons that had touched him were taken to the sick, and their illnesses were cured and the evil spirits left them.¹³ Some Jews who went around driving out evil spirits tried to invoke the name of the Lord Jesus over those who were demon-possessed. They would say, "In the name of the Jesus whom Paul preaches, I command you to come out." ¹⁴ Seven sons of Sceva, a Jewish chief priest, were doing this.* $^{15}$ *One day the evil spirit answered them, "Jesus I know, and Paul I know about, but who are you?"* $^{16}$ *Then the man who had the evil spirit jumped on them and overpowered them all. He gave them such a beating that they ran out of the house naked and bleeding.*

## Luke 22:39-46

*39Jesus went out as usual to the Mount of Olives, and his disciples followed him. 40On reaching the place, he said to them, "Pray that you will not fall into temptation." 41He withdrew about a stone's throw beyond them, knelt down and prayed, 42"Father, if you are willing, take this cup from me; yet not my will, but yours be done." 43An angel from heaven appeared to him and strengthened him. 44And being in anguish, he prayed more earnestly, and his sweat was like drops of blood falling to the ground. 45When he rose from prayer and went back to the disciples, he found them asleep, exhausted from sorrow. 46"Why are you sleeping?" he asked them. "Get up and pray so that you will not fall into temptation."*

## Matthew 26:36-46

$^{36}$ *Then Jesus went with them to a place called Gethsemane, and he said to his disciples, "Sit here, while I go over there and pray."* $^{37}$ *And taking with him Peter and the two sons of Zebedee, he began to be sorrowful and troubled. ³⁸ Then he said to them, "My soul is very sorrowful, even to death; remain here, and watch with me." ³⁹ And going a little farther he fell on his face and prayed, saying, "My Father, if it be possible, let this cup pass from me; nevertheless, not as I will, but as you will." ⁴⁰ And he came to the disciples and found them sleeping. And he said to Peter, "So, could you not watch with me one hour? ⁴¹ Watch and pray that you may not enter into temptation. The spirit indeed is willing, but the flesh is weak." ⁴² Again, for the second time, he went away and prayed, "My Father, if this cannot pass unless I drink it, your will be done." ⁴³ And again he came and found them sleeping, for their eyes were heavy. ⁴⁴ So, leaving them again, he went away and prayed for the third time, saying the same words again. ⁴⁵ Then he came to the disciples and said to them, "Sleep and take your rest later on. See, the hour is at hand, and the Son of Man is betrayed into the hands of sinners. ⁴⁶ Rise, let us be going; see, my betrayer is at hand."*

So, what exactly is the press? The press is when you are in a throng of thousands of people all trying to get a piece of Jesus and you, although you are weak in your body, you push yourself past your physical limitations, you stretch yourself until you can touch the very tip, the hem of His garment. The woman with the issue of blood is pressing in the natural dimension but she got her breakthrough in the supernatural dimension.

When you press you wrestle in the realm of the spirit. You'll go all night long if you have too. You'll be exactly like Jacob still praying at daybreak, saying, "I won't let go until Heaven blesses me." When you wrestle with the unseen forces in this way, you develop spiritual muscle. You gain a new name. You're not just some regular guy named Jacob anymore. One who came to God representing his small-town views and selfish ideas. You gain a new name in the press and a new perspective. You're not small-time anymore either. You've become a nation. When you press your way past demonic powers and principalities to have an encounter with God, everything and everybody in the spirit realm will know your name.

When you press you gain the very thing that the sons of the local high priest, did not have. The seven sons of Sceva saw people in their city who were demonically oppressed. They thought they could ride in on their father's anointing and save the day. But the demons didn't know their names in the realm of the spirit, because, unlike Paul, the seven sons of Sceva had built no fame nor spiritual muscle because they had not been in the press.

The press is when despite having obtained no justice you keep going back and forth to court. The widow of Luke 18 was going to court in the temporal realm, but she received her victory in the supernatural realm. Why? Well, because she had the wherewithal and the good presence of mind to keep pressing. The widow received victory because victory is a bi-product of the press.

The woman with the issue of blood received her healing because deliverance from the things that ail us is a bi-product of the press. Jacob received a new name because fame, great exploits and a new name are all results of the press. Jesus fought past the desires of his own flesh and went to the cross, endured the worst torture that any human being will ever have to go through, because the power to walk out your destiny comes from the press. I don't know about you, but I'm so glad He pressed. I don't know where I would be right now had the Savior of the world not submitted Himself to the press. This is a great place for me to go ahead and interject principle number 4:

# PRINCIPLE #4

## VICTORY IS A BY-PRODUCT OF THE PRESS. DELIVERANCE IS A BY-PRODUCT OF THE PRESS. FAME IS A BY-PRODUCT OF THE PRESS. THE POWER TO WALK INTO PURPOSE AND DESTINY COMES WHEN YOU SUBMIT YOURSELF TO THE PRESS.

Now you might be saying to yourself right now, "Those were some great scriptures but what exactly are the mechanics of the press? How do I do it? What do I need to enter into the press?" Well the first thing you need is violence.

## Matthew 11:12

*And from the days of John the Baptist until now the kingdom of heaven suffers violence, and the violent take it by force.*

You see, according to Matthew 11:12 we cannot lay hold of the kingdom without it. The press represents violent prayer. It's intentional intensity. It's the type of prayer Jesus prayed in the garden. According to Luke 22, Jesus pressed himself to a place in prayer that he experienced a physical reaction in his body. Jesus provides for us the perfect example. The press requires us to push past ourselves, spiritually, mentally and physically.

## Jude 1:20

[20] *But you, dear friends, by building yourselves up in your most holy faith and praying in the Holy Spirit,*

## Ephesians 6:10-18

[10] *Finally, be strong in the Lord and in his mighty power.* [11] *Put on the full armor of God, so that you*

*can take your stand against the devil's schemes.* *¹² For our struggle is not against flesh and blood, but against the rulers, against the authorities, against the powers of this dark world and against the spiritual forces of evil in the heavenly realms. ¹³ Therefore put on the full armor of God, so that when the day of evil comes, you may be able to stand your ground, and after you have done everything, to stand. ¹⁴ Stand firm then, with the belt of truth buckled around your waist, with the breastplate of righteousness in place, ¹⁵ and with your feet fitted with the readiness that comes from the gospel of peace. ¹⁶ In addition to all this, take up the shield of faith, with which you can extinguish all the flaming arrows of the evil one. ¹⁷ Take the helmet of salvation and the sword of the Spirit, which is the word of God. ¹⁸ And pray in the Spirit on all occasions with all kinds of prayers and requests. With this in mind, be alert and always keep on praying for all the Lord's people.*

## Romans 8:26-27

*²⁶ In the same way, the Spirit helps us in our weakness. We do not know what we ought to pray for, but the Spirit himself intercedes for us through wordless groans. ²⁷ And he who searches our hearts knows the mind of the Spirit, because the Spirit intercedes for God's people in accordance with the will of God.*

The next thing you will need to effectively enter the press is a fabulous tool that I think every intercessor should have at their disposal, called praying in the Spirit. Praying in the Spirit is one of the easiest ways to enter into the press and according to Ephesians 6, it is the last piece of the armor. Like every other piece of the armor, your prayer language will protect you.

When you pray in the spirit you pray what I like to call, bulls-eye prayers. We all know what a bulls-eye prayer is, don't we? It's a prayer that hits the mark every single time. Romans 8 tells us that we don't even know how to pray. We miss the mark time and time again. We pray our will instead of His will. Sometimes we pray out of our emotions instead of out of our spirits. However, the apostle Paul says that the Holy Spirit helps us in our human frailties and weakness by interceding through us with wordless groans. Paul is referring here to the prayer language which makes absolutely no sense to the natural ear, but in the realm of the Spirit where both God and the evil one abides, it is the language of Heaven. It is the effectual fervent prayer of the righteous man that avails much.

In my travels I meet many different types of believers. I've met believers who tell me that they have a prayer language, but they can't use it any time they want to. They must wait for the stirring of the Holy Spirit in order to use their language to pray. Beloved, if you learned your native language as a small child and then, suddenly, you couldn't use your voice to speak for some reason, we would recognize that as a mental and or psychological problem. Same in the spirit. If you can't speak in your heavenly language whenever you need to, there is a problem. It's a sign of a broken and or malnourished spirit man. I've also met believers who received their prayer language early on in their Christian walk, but who only use it from time to time. If the enemy only comes to make war against you, and your loved ones from time to time, then I guess that a time to time prayer language will suffice. However, if Satan is waging war on you and or the people you love on a regular basis, well, then you might want to pull out this very important tool. When you pray in the spirit language the enemy can't decode your prayers.

Have you ever had the experience of praying a prayer in English (or your native language if English isn't your native tongue) and it seemed like the very opposite of what you prayed began to happen? Satan knows that the moment you start praying God starts moving for you, so he sends reinforcements out to fight against the very thing that you are praying for. These satanic reinforcements cause the blessings of God to be delayed, and when the people of God become despondent and lose hope, these demonic reinforcements cause the people of God to forfeit the blessings of God all together. When we pray in the spirit we devil proof our prayers. If the enemy can't decipher your prayers he certainly can't stop them. And don't let the people of God come together corporately and begin to pray in unknown tongues. watch out, boy! The enemy really hates this. Why?

Because alarms begin to sound in the spirit as the people of God begin to breach his walls. Bombs begin to explode throughout his kingdom. Heavenly officers of the King of Kings high court show up with subpoenas in hand, and key principalities in Satan's organization are hauled into court for emergency hearings. As the people of God bombard the courts of heaven with their prayers, pardons are handed down in the realm of the spirit. Prison doors swing open. The enemy stands by and watches helplessly as prisoners who have been bound for years go free. My description really doesn't do it justice. The Prophet Joel said it best. He spoke about this powerful prayer army and the havoc that is created in the spiritual realm when they go forth:

## Joel 2:1-11

*Blow the trumpet in Zion;*
  *sound the alarm on my holy hill.*
*Let all who live in the land tremble,*
  *for the day of the* LORD *is coming.*
*It is close at hand—*
*2  a day of darkness and gloom,*
  *a day of clouds and blackness.*
*Like dawn spreading across the mountains*
  *a large and mighty army comes,*
*such as never was in ancient times*
  *nor ever will be in ages to come.*
*3 Before them fire devours,*
  *behind them a flame blazes.*
*Before them the land is like the garden of Eden,*
  *behind them, a desert waste—*

*nothing escapes them.*
*⁴ They have the appearance of horses;*
*they gallop along like cavalry.*
*⁵ With a noise like that of chariots*
*they leap over the mountaintops,*
*like a crackling fire consuming stubble,*
*like a mighty army drawn up for battle.*
*⁶ At the sight of them, nations are in anguish;*
*every face turns pale.*
*⁷ They charge like warriors;*
*they scale walls like soldiers.*
*They all march in line,*
*not swerving from their course.*
*⁸ They do not jostle each other;*
*each marches straight ahead.*
*They plunge through defenses*
*without breaking ranks.*
*⁹ They rush upon the city;*
*they run along the wall.*
*They climb into the houses;*
*like thieves they enter through the windows.* *¹⁰ Before them the earth shakes,*
*the heavens tremble,*
*the sun and moon are darkened,*
*and the stars no longer shine.*
*¹¹ The L*ORD *thunders*
*at the head of his army;*
*his forces are beyond number,*
*and mighty is the army that obeys his command.*
*The day of the L*ORD *is great;*
*it is dreadful.*
*Who can endure it?*

Did you catch the fact that The Lord Himself is at the helm of this army? He is the leader of this army as they pray by His Spirit. Joel 2 is a picture of what happens when believers come together corporately and everyone pulls their own weight. They are all active participants in the prayer. Not passive. If Joel 2 is a picture of the people of God getting it right, then Nehemiah 3 is a picture of the people of God getting it wrong.

## Nehemiah 3: 3-5

*The Fish Gate was rebuilt by the sons of Hassenaah. They laid its beams and put its doors and bolts and bars in place. [4] Meremoth son of Uriah, the son of Hakkoz, repaired the next section. Next to him Meshullam son of Berekiah, the son of Meshezabel, made repairs, and next to him Zadok son of Baana also made repairs. [5] The next section was repaired by the men of Tekoa, but their nobles would not put their shoulders to the work under their supervisors.*

This is a written account of who built the wall. By now I'm sure we all understand that the wall is symbolic for prayer. I want you to notice verse five. The scripture makes it a point to call out the nobles of Tekoa. We can all probably guess who the nobles were right? These were the prominent folks in the community. The most esteemed. Scripture calls them out for two reasons. Number 1: they wouldn't do any heavy lifting in the spirit realm and Number 2: they wouldn't submit to the building supervisors. The folks who built walls every day.

Sometimes we think we know how to go in and touch God because we are a pastor or bishop. But there are regular everyday folks who sit in the pews Sunday after Sunday without titles who have the wherewithal to go up in the realm of the spirit and touch God's heart. But the nobles won't submit to their leadership.

And let's not forget about those church leaders who want to regulate prayer to the intercessory prayer team. This is a huge mistake because as we see in the Joel chapter, God is at the head of His army. He is the Commander and He gives direction and intel to generals. God speaks to generals. You don't send your administrative assistant out to meet the Commander of the Army. You talk to Him yourself. Abraham was rich in cattle, servants and land, but when the King of Glory stopped by his house that day, he didn't call for one of his servants to serve Him. Abraham waited on God himself.

Let's take a look at the terminology used in verse 5. It says that they wouldn't put their shoulders to the work. That's not to say that they weren't praying at all, it means they weren't pressing. I know they weren't pressing because the press is physical. In other words, you've got to put your whole body into the press. Any woman who has ever birthed a child from their body will tell you that although the baby comes out of one part, every part of your body has got to press that baby out. This shoulder terminology is important because of another reason, the mantle.

Every leader has a mantle. Go ahead and wrap your brain around that statement for a second. Doesn't matter what you are called to lead, you have a mantle for it. If you're called to lead your church softball team you have a mantle for it. And if it's getting too hard for you to do the thing that God has called you to do, perhaps you are drawing off your own strength and not utilizing the power available to you in your mantle.

In Biblical days, the mantle would tie around the neck and extend over the shoulders. The person's rank and position determined how long the train on the mantle was. The train was a physical representation of the person's spiritual authority. Isaiah tells us that one day he was serving in the temple and he saw the Lord, high and lifted up, and he said that His train was so long that it filled the entire Temple. Wow, no one has authority like that!

For the most part the people of God don't wear physical mantles anymore, but in the invisible realm, trust and believe, the mantle is still there. The mantle acts as your spiritual covering and it endows you with power to lead. So, what this verse is really saying is that these leaders refused to lend their mantles (or their supernatural strength) to the building process. When leaders lend their mantles to prayer, things can be accomplished in the spirit realm quickly just by the virtue of the sheer weight they carry in the spiritual realm.

†

# CHAPTER FIVE
# BACKLASH & RETALIATION

It never fails, whenever a great victory is won, all hell breaks loose. Intercessors refer to this phenomenon as backlash and retaliation. I think backlash and retaliation requires a chapter of its own, because of the posture that the people of God take in relationship to it. I've actually met Christians who will not participate in any type of spiritual warfare at all because of fear of receiving backlash and retaliation from the kingdom of darkness. In the first passage in this chapter, we will be looking at the Apostle Paul and his traveling companion Silas who find themselves in prison because of some backlash and retaliation.

## Acts 16: 16-24

*[16] Once when we were going to the place of prayer, we were met by a female slave who had a spirit by which she predicted the future. She earned a great deal of money for her owners by fortune-telling. [17] She followed Paul and the rest of us, shouting, "These men are servants of the Most High God, who are telling you the way to be saved." [18] She kept this up for many days. Finally Paul became so annoyed that he turned around and said to the spirit, "In the name of Jesus Christ I command you to come out of her!" At that moment the spirit left her. [19] When her*

*owners realized that their hope of making money was gone, they seized Paul and Silas and dragged them into the marketplace to face the authorities. [20] They brought them before the magistrates and said, "These men are Jews, and are throwing our city into an uproar [21] by advocating customs unlawful for us Romans to accept or practice."[22] The crowd joined in the attack against Paul and Silas, and the magistrates ordered them to be stripped and beaten with rods. [23] After they had been severely flogged, they were thrown into prison, and the jailer was commanded to guard them carefully. [24] When he received these orders, he put them in the inner cell and fastened their feet in the stocks.*

Now, Paul had, certainly prior to this episode performed deliverance on several other occasions. According to the demon that beat the seven sons of Sceva, Paul was not only internationally known he was supernaturally known as well. And yet there was something about him casting the demon out of the slave girl in the passage we just read that caused the enemy to double back and strike him. Paul didn't just merely set a slave woman free, he struck a blow to this city's economic power base. This isn't ground level warfare any more, Paul attacked the system, and the principalities over that region struck back. Let's see how Paul and Silas dealt with this backlash and retaliation.

## Acts 16: 25-31

*$^{25}$ But at midnight Paul and Silas were praying and singing hymns to God, and the prisoners were listening to them. $^{26}$ Suddenly there was a great earthquake, so that the foundations of the prison were shaken; and immediately all the doors were opened and everyone's chains were loosed. $^{27}$ And the keeper of the prison, awaking from sleep and seeing the prison doors open, supposing the prisoners had fled, drew his sword and was about to kill himself. $^{28}$ But Paul called with a loud voice, saying, "Do yourself no harm, for we are all here."$^{29}$ Then he called for a light, ran in, and fell down trembling before Paul and Silas. $^{30}$ And he brought them out and said, "Sirs, what must I do to be saved?"$^{31}$ So they said, "Believe on the Lord Jesus Christ, and you will be saved, you and your household."*

Scripture says that around midnight, Paul and Silas mounted a counter attack. They were chained up together in prison. Praying and praising God with a sincere heart, when suddenly, there was a great earthquake. Every jail cell flew open and every prisoner's chains fell off. Wow! What a way to deal with backlash. Hear me people of God, if you respond to backlash and retaliation the right way, not only will you break free but everyone else around you will break free as well. Paul and Silas chose to worship and give thanks instead of wringing their hands in fear.

## Acts 28: 1-6

*Once safely on shore, we found out that the island was called Malta. 2The islanders showed us unusual kindness. They built a fire and welcomed us all because it was raining and cold. 3Paul gathered a pile of brushwood and, as he put it on the fire, a viper, driven out by the heat, fastened itself on his hand. 4When the islanders saw the snake hanging from his hand, they said to each other, "This man must be a murderer; for though he escaped from the sea, the goddess Justice has not allowed him to live." 5But Paul shook the snake off into the fire and suffered no ill effects. 6The people expected him to swell up or suddenly fall dead; but after waiting a long time and seeing nothing unusual happen to him, they changed their minds and said he was a god.*

Once again, we see that a snake bit him and what did he do? He shook it off.

## Mark 16:17-18

*17And these signs will accompany those who believe: In my name they will drive out demons; they will speak in new tongues; 18they will pick up snakes with their hands; and when they drink deadly poison, it will not hurt them at all; they will place their hands on sick people, and they will get well."*

Notice that verse 18 states, "when they consume poison," not if they consume poison. Now this is not an excuse to be foolish. I recently heard a story about a pastor who was handling deadly snakes in a service because he was standing on this particular passage in scripture. What do you think happened to that man? He was bitten and he dropped dead right in the middle of the church service. The letter of the law kills but the Spirit gives life.

## James 1:12

*Blessed is the one who perseveres under trial because, having stood the test, that person will receive the crown of life that the Lord has promised to those who love him.*

## Revelation 2:10-11

*Do not be afraid of what you are about to suffer. I tell you, the devil will put some of you in prison to test you, and you will suffer persecution for ten days. Be faithful, even to the point of death, and I will give you life as your victor's crown.* [11] *Whoever has ears, let them hear what the Spirit says to the churches. The one who is victorious will not be hurt at all by the second death.*

## Nehemiah 4:7-9

*But when Sanballat, Tobiah, the Arabs, the Ammonites and the people of Ashdod heard that the repairs to Jerusalem's walls had gone ahead and that the gaps were being closed, they were very angry. <sup>8</sup> They all plotted together to come and fight against Jerusalem and stir up trouble against it. <sup>9</sup> But we prayed to our God and posted a guard day and night to meet this threat.*

## Nehemiah 4: 11-12

*Also our enemies said before they know it or see us we will be right there among them and will kill them and put an end to the work. Then the Jews who lived near them came and told us ten times over, wherever you turn they will attack us.*

I've met people of God who have said I don't want to move into the ministry of intercession because they say: when I do, something always happens to the people in my family. That is the mindset of a defeated Christian. Let me tell you what Nehemiah did to deal with backlash and retaliation. Let's read the next verse together.

## Nehemiah 4:13

*¹³ Therefore I stationed some of the people behind the lowest points of the wall at the exposed places, posting them by families, with their swords, spears and bows.*

What's he saying in that verse? He's saying, that he sured up the weak places! You know the weak places in your wall, beloved. Every family has them, every ministry has them, every race and people group on the planet has them. Maybe it's your unsaved mother, or your alcoholic sister. It could be systemic poverty or violence that has ravaged your bloodline. But I stand on that word you just read in Acts 16, for every one of my wayward family members. If you believe on the Lord Jesus, you and your whole household will be saved. My adult brother doesn't live in my physical house, and, yet and still, I count him as part of my household because I'm the one who covers him spiritually in prayer. I'm the kinsman redeemer for my bloodline and he is my territory.

Backlash and retaliation are unfortunate realities for anyone moving in purpose and destiny. Still, if you can respond correctly, you, and everyone around you can break free. Let the enemy rattle your cage, let him expose all the weak, and broken places along your wall. Then mount up and fight back. I tell my intercessors: we eat backlash and retaliation for breakfast. Fried backlash and smothered retaliation. Funny yes, but what am I really saying? We are not afraid. We are of them who will not draw back because healing and deliverance is our birthright. Which brings me to principle number five. It's a declaration so say it out loud with me:

# PRINCIPLE # 5

**WE DON'T FEAR BACKLASH AND RETALIATION. WE EAT IT FOR BREAKFAST: FRIED BACKLASH AND SMOTHERED RETALIATION.**

✝

# CHAPTER SIX
# AVENGERS & REDEEMERS

## Ruth 3:7-9

*⁷ When Boaz had finished eating and drinking and was in good spirits, he went over to lie down at the far end of the grain pile. Ruth approached quietly, uncovered his feet and lay down. ⁸ In the middle of the night something startled the man; he turned—and there was a woman lying at his feet! ⁹ "Who are you?" he asked. "I am your servant Ruth," she said. "Spread the corner of your garment over me, since you are a guardian-redeemer of our family."*

## Ruth 4:1-12

*Meanwhile Boaz went up to the town gate and sat down there just as the guardian-redeemer he had mentioned came along. Boaz said, "Come over here, my friend, and sit down." So he went over and sat down. ² Boaz took ten of the elders of the town and said, "Sit here," and they did so. ³ Then he said to the guardian-redeemer, "Naomi, who has come back from Moab, is selling the piece of land that belonged to our relative Elimelek. ⁴ I thought I should bring the matter to your attention and suggest that you buy it in the presence of these seated here and in the presence of the elders of my people. If you will redeem it, do so. But if you will not, tell me, so I will know. For no one has the right to do it except you, and I am next in line." "I will redeem it," he said. ⁵ Then Boaz said, "On the day you buy the land from Naomi, you also acquire Ruth the Moabite, the dead man's widow, in order to maintain the name of the dead with his property." ⁶ At this, the guardian-redeemer said, "Then I cannot redeem it because I might endanger my own estate. You redeem it yourself. I cannot do it." ⁷ (Now in earlier times in Israel, for the redemption and transfer of property to become final, one party took off his sandal and gave it to the other. This was the method of legalizing transactions in Israel.) ⁸ So the guardian-redeemer said to Boaz, "Buy it yourself." And he removed his sandal.*

*⁹ Then Boaz announced to the elders and all the people, "Today you are witnesses that I have bought from Naomi all the property of Elimelek, Kilion and Mahlon. ¹⁰ I have also acquired Ruth the Moabite, Mahlon's widow, as my wife, in order to maintain the name of the dead with his property, so that his name will not disappear from among his family or from his hometown. Today you are witnesses!" ¹¹ Then the elders and all the people at the gate said, "We are witnesses. May the LORD make the woman who is coming into your home like Rachel and Leah, who together built up the family of Israel. May you have standing in Ephrathah and be famous in Bethlehem. ¹² Through the offspring the LORD gives you by this young woman, may your family be like that of Perez, whom Tamar bore to Judah."*

I don't have time to tell the whole story but here's the Cliff Notes version. Naomi, a Jewish woman, and her family move to the land of Moab because of a famine in Israel. During her sojourn in Moab, her husband and both of her sons die. She's got herself and two daughter- in- laws left. That's it. Ruth and Orpah. She tells them that according to Jewish custom, they are supposed to wait and become the wives of her next sons but, "Let's face it, I'm an old woman. I won't be having any more children, so I bless you and I release you from any familial debt you have to me." Naomi tells her daughters-in-law to go home. They both cry and say, "No-no. It wouldn't be right for us to leave you destitute and alone." Naomi is very bitter about her situation, and she insists saying, "Look, can't you see that the Almighty One is against me? I left my country full, now I'm going back home empty. Go back to your people and to your gods." Orpah says, "Well, since you put it like that, deuces, gotta go." But Ruth says, "Where you go I will go. Your God will be my God and your people my people."

This is a very dangerous position for a woman to be in during this particular time in history. She has no man to serve as her covering and it's against the law for her to own property. In fact, many of the prostitutes in Israel at the time were widows who had no sons, just like Naomi. When Boaz tells the kinsmen there's a piece of property Naomi wants to sell. Understand that she's selling it because, legally, she can't own it herself. This is the absolute worst time in history to be a woman and yet Naomi returns to her homeland during harvest time. Ruth happens to find day work in the field of a man named Boaz, a close relative of Naomi's deceased husband. Boaz shows Ruth the kind of kindness that makes Naomi believe he may have the heart to redeem. Ruth is an outsider. She is a foreigner. She is a Moabite, and most likely her skin was dark. She is most likely of African descent. But Boaz knows a little bit about being an outsider too. His mother is Rahab the prostitute who hid the spies.

Naomi carefully instructs her daughter as to what to say and what to do. Ruth goes to the threshing floor and makes her proposal. Boaz is flattered by her offer. He tells her that there is a closer relative and that that man has the right to redeem her first. But if he doesn't agree to do it, Boaz says that he will surely redeem her. This closer relative was interested in the property but not in the responsibility that came along with it. Taking the property meant he'd have to marry Ruth. It also meant that the first child Ruth conceived would not be considered his son at all. This child would actually be considered the son of Ruth's dead husband. Thus, the land that the redeemer had purchased with his own hard earned cash would go to another man's heir. So he says, "Nope, can't do it."

We know the rest of the story. Ruth marries Boaz and becomes the mother of Obed who was the father of

Jesse. Who was the Father of David. Jesus would come through the line of David, and He would be the ultimate kinsman redeemer. But what I want you to see is that from the very beginning of Israel's formation as a nation God placed kinsman redeemers in every family. These were people who realized they were blessed to be a blessing to others. God never intended for His people to return back to slavery, so He set kinsman redeemers in every family as a safeguard to keep this from happening. If you fell on hard times the job of the kinsman redeemer was to buy you and your property back. Then hold it in trust for you until you could get your act together. And, in the case of a woman who was left without a husband, the kinsman redeemer's job was to marry her and provide an heir. But just like today, redemption bares with it a heavy cost and everybody wasn't willing to pay it.

## Numbers 35: 16-21

*[16] "'If anyone strikes someone a fatal blow with an iron object, that person is a murderer; the murderer is to be put to death. [17] Or if anyone is holding a stone and strikes someone a fatal blow with it, that person is a murderer; the murderer is to be put to death. [18] Or if anyone is holding a wooden object and strikes someone a fatal blow with it, that person is a murderer; the murderer is to be put to death. [19] The avenger of blood shall put the murderer to death; when the avenger comes upon the murderer, the*

*avenger shall put the murderer to death.* [20] *If anyone with malice aforethought shoves another or throws something at them intentionally so that they die* [21] *or if out of enmity one person hits another with their fist so that the other dies, that person is to be put to death; that person is a murderer. The avenger of blood shall put the murderer to death when they meet.*

The blood avenger is that crazy family member your grandma calls when something foul goes down in the family. He's not certifiably crazy per say . . . but everyone knows you ought to stay out of his way. Well, in biblical days, this person was not insane; they were bound by honor and duty to avenge a family members death, vigilante style. Every family had them. If you took the life of one of their family members. Then the avenger had the legal right to come after you. This is actually one of the roles of the kinsman redeemer. Not only would he buy you out of slavery, he would destroy anything or anybody that came to destroy you.

## Psalm 8: 1-2

*L ORD, our Lord, how majestic is your name in all the earth! You have set your glory in the heavens.* [2] *Through the praise of children and infants you have established a stronghold against your enemies, to silence the foe and the avenger.*

I love this scripture. It's definitely one of my top ten scriptures as it relates to prayer. I love this scripture because of all the secrets encoded inside of it. There is so much strength found in these two verses. First, it tells us the value of praise. Not just any praise. Pure childlike praise. You don't have to be a professional to do this. You don't have to be on the worship team to do this. You don't even have to be a mature saint to comprehend this. You can be a babe sucking on milk. You just have to have the heart of a child. This is some, them- that- worship- Him- in- Spirit- and- in- truth- stuff. It tells you the value of this kind of praise. You can establish a stronghold with it.

Another word for stronghold is a heavily fortified castle, a city, or a fortress. This fortress that has been established by your pure praise will silence both the foe and the avenger. Now the foe he's just your natural born enemy. He hates you because you live and because you name the name of Christ and you are born of the Adamic race. But the psalmist is writing for an audience that understands Jewish law. And according to Jewish law, the avenger is the one who has a right to destroy you. The priest of God actually set cities of refuge aside in Israel to protect innocent people from the avenger.

But the passage here tells us that our pure childlike praise can form a city to protect us from the one who has the right to attack us. Wow! I don't know about you, but I know I've done some things that have given the devil the right to come after me. And I am most grateful for a way of escape. Psalm 8 tells me that my praise can build a city. The last thing that Psalm 8:1-2 tells me is that there are still avengers in the land. But their battle is not against flesh and blood. We fight against a supernatural enemy. And because our enemy is supernatural, God has given us a supernatural tool to fight him. He told us to open our mouths and praise Him. Which leads me to principle number six:

# PRINCIPLE #6

## GOD IS A GOD OF FAMILIES AND LEGACIES. HE IS A GOD OF GENERATIONS. HE STILL NEEDS KINSMAN REDEEMERS IN THE EARTH

God doesn't change His mind. Kinsman redeemers and blood avengers were a good idea then and as far as He's concerned they are still a good idea now. These are people who have been given both natural and supernatural resources to buy their relatives out of slavery. Could that person be you? Are you called to buy your family out of bondage and break generational curses? Are you willing to pay the price? I believe that Moses was a kinsman redeemer for Israel. I believe that Harriet Tubman was a kinsman redeemer for black people in America. Did you know the generational curse of child molestation will run for sixteen generations unless somebody stands up in the family as a kinsman redeemer/blood avenger and breaks the curse? God is looking for some kinsman redeemers to stand in the gap.

# INTERCESSION
# The Heart Beat of God

# Part III

**The Role of the Intercessor**

**Governmental Intercession**

**Intimacy & Authority**

✝

# CHAPTER SEVEN
# The Role of the Intercessor

In this chapter we are going to deviate from our current format just a bit. You may remember me telling you, at the beginning of this study, that this book was based on a course that I used to teach entitled, *The Role of the Intercessor*. Well, think of this chapter as that course on steroids. So not only am I going to give you a principle as it relates to prayer, I am also going to give you ten duties, all gathered from scripture that when put together, give us a great understanding of the role of the intercessor. Are you ready. Let's begin.

### Role #1 The Role of the Intercessor is to:

### **BE THE GATE & GUARD THE GATES**

### John 10: 1-3

*Very truly I tell you Pharisees, anyone who does not enter the sheep pen by the gate, but climbs in by some other way, is a thief and a robber. 2The one who* *enters by the gate is the shepherd of the sheep. 3**The gatekeeper opens the gate for him, and the sheep listen to his voice**. He calls his own sheep by name and leads them out.*

Go ahead and declare the following statements with me:

1. I'm a gatekeeper.
2. I'm a gatekeeper in the house of the Lord.
3. I am a gatekeeper in my family.
4. I am a gatekeeper in my city.
5. I am a gatekeeper in my community.
6. I stand on the wall of my nation.

Now when we talk about gates in this context, we aren't talking about that chain linked fence that you put up in the backyard last summer. We are talking about spiritual portals located throughout the earth. A huge part of guarding the gates, is making sure that they are open for the King of Glory to come in. We do that by setting the atmosphere wherever we go. By charging the atmosphere with praise and worship. By arresting the atmosphere and making it conducive to the move of God's Spirit. In order to guard the gates effectively, as an intercessor, you must be sensitive to but not sensitized by the environment around you.

When you are sensitized by the environment, whatever is going on in the environment causes you to react in a negative way. Another way to say this is to say, that you had an allergic reaction to what's going on around you. On the other hand, when you are sensitive to the environment, you are quick to detect or respond to slight atmospheric pressures or influences around you. When you are sensitive, you respond in the correct way. You become thoughtful, tactful. You respond in a way that is wise as serpents but gentle as doves. For example, you might sense death in the room, but you ain't taking it home with you. In fact, you will arrest it and make sure no one else takes it home either. The role of the intercessor is to guard the gates.

## Psalms 24:7-10

*$^7$ Lift up your heads, you gates; be lifted up, you ancient doors, that the King of glory may come in. $^8$ Who is this King of glory? The L<small>ORD</small> strong and mighty, the L<small>ORD</small> mighty in battle. $^9$ Lift up your heads, you gates; lift them up, you ancient doors, that the King of glory may come in. $^{10}$ Who is he, this King of glory? The L<small>ORD</small> Almighty—he is the King of glory.*


This scripture verse is one of what I call the 24/7s. The scripture gives us some useful instruction and its location in scripture tells us how often we are supposed to do it—24/7. All the time. This passage tells us something very important about both ourselves and God. In the John passages above you learned that you were a gatekeeper. Here in Psalm 24 you learn that you are a gate.

Go ahead and say that out loud: **I am a gate**. I can lay hands on the sick and they will recover because I am a gate. Anything that comes into this earth realm must come in through a gate. If deliverance, or justice, or peace, or healing, or miracles, forgiveness, or mercy will enter the land it must come through me the gate. The role of the intercessor is to be the gate and to guard the gates.

## Role #2 The Role of the Intercessor is to:

## RECOGNIZE THE THIEF & COMMAND RECOMPENSE

## John 10:10

*10The thief comes only to steal and kill and destroy; I have come that they may have life, and have it to the full.*

## Proverbs 6:30-31

*People do not despise a thief if he steals to satisfy his hunger when he is starving. 31Yet if he is caught, he must pay sevenfold, though it costs him all the wealth of his house.*

## Acts 16:16-18

*Once when we were going to the place of prayer, we were met by a slave girl who had a spirit by which she predicted the future. She earned a great deal of money for her owners by fortune-telling. This girl followed Paul and the rest of us shouting These men are servants of the Most High God, who are telling you the way to be saved. She kept this up for many days. Finally Paul became so troubled that he turned around and said to the spirit, in the name of Jesus Christ I command you to come out of her! At that moment the spirit left her.*


Your job is to recognize the thief. To bring charges against the enemy in the courts of heaven. To command a sevenfold return. That word simply means complete recovery. And to not allow him to steal anything else again. That means that as an intercessor, you are supposed to arrest demonic doctrines that come across the pulpits. In churches all over the world, and particularly America, doctrines of devils creep in. I'm not talking about false teachings which are a lot more blatant in nature. I'm talking about the little foxes that spoil the vine. The ungodly mixture of a little bit of truth with a dash of a lie. This is what Paul was contending with in Acts 16. The woman following them was saying all the right stuff. Yet something about it was off. This was a doctrine of devils.

Let's talk about that Acts passage for a moment. There is a lot of instability that hangs out among the prophets and the intercessors. Beloved, don't believe every spirit, try the spirit and see if it be of God. There are many voices speaking in the spirit realm. If God is always telling you somebody else's business, it may not be the spirit of God. You may have a spirit from which you need to be delivered. Let's read the next passage together:

## Luke 16:19-26

*"There was a rich man who was dressed in purple and fine linen and lived in luxury every day. $^{20}$ At his gate was laid a beggar named Lazarus, covered with sores $^{21}$ and longing to eat what fell from the rich man's table. Even the dogs came and licked his sores.$^{22}$ "The time came when the beggar died and the angels carried him to Abraham's side. The rich man also died and was buried. $^{23}$ In Hades, where he was in torment, he looked up and saw Abraham far away, with Lazarus by his side. $^{24}$ So he called to him, 'Father Abraham, have pity on me and send Lazarus to dip the tip of his finger in water and cool my tongue, because I am in agony in this fire.' $^{25}$ "But Abraham replied, 'Son, remember that in your*

*lifetime you received your good things, while Lazarus received bad things, but now he is comforted here and you are in agony. $^{26}$ And besides all this, between us and you a great chasm has been set in place, so that those who want to go from here to you cannot, nor can anyone cross over from there to us.'*

If you see in the spirit realm and there is no gulf or chasm between you and what you see, you may be in need of some deliverance. The young woman in Acts wasn't super-spiritual, she was just plain freaky. Furthermore, you don't have to tell everyone everything you see. Use discernment.


There is a true story I like to tell about the freedom fighter, Harriet Tubman. Through the aid of a lawyer she found out that her mother's freedom had been stolen from her. Her previous master had written in his will that, upon his death, she was to be freed. That meant that all of the children born to her afterward would also be free, because according to the slave laws at the time, slave children followed the condition of the mother, not the father. So not only had this man stolen her mother's freedom but he had also stolen the freedom of Harriet and all her siblings. She said when she found out about this she hated this man. But God spoke to her heart and told her to forgive him and to pray for him every day. Harriet said as she prayed for this man she felt the bitterness in her heart melt away. That man, her master died painfully and mysteriously and Harriet Tubman went on to make nineteen trips to the south and escort over

300 people to freedom. For the freedom that was stolen from her, God recompensed her and gave her so many more lives. Now the man who stole from her nobody remembers his name. But everybody remembers Harriet Tubman, the Moses of the South. The role of the intercessor is to: recognize the thief and command recompense.

## Role #3 The Role of the Intercessor is to:

## **BE QUIET & INSPECT THE LAND**

## Nehemiah 2 11-18

11. I went to Jerusalem, and after staying there three *days. 12 I set out during the night with a few others. I had not told anyone what my God had put in my heart to do for Jerusalem. There were no mounts with me except the one I was riding on.13By night I went out through the Valley Gate toward the Jackal Well and the Dung Gate, examining the walls of Jerusalem, which had been broken down, and its gates, which had been destroyed by fire. 14Then I moved on toward the Fountain Gate and the King's Pool, but there was not enough room for my mount to get through; 15so I went up the valley by night, examining the wall. Finally, I turned back and reentered through the Valley Gate. 16The officials did not know where I had gone or what I was doing,*

*because as yet I had said nothing to the Jews or the priests or nobles or officials or any others who would be doing the work 17Then I said to them, "You see the trouble we are in: Jerusalem lies in ruins, and its gates have been burned with fire. Come, let us rebuild the wall of Jerusalem, and we will no longer be in disgrace." 18I also told them about the gracious hand of my God on me and what the king had said to me. They replied, "Let us start rebuilding." So they began this good work.*

## Matthew 6:5-14

*⁵ "And when you pray, do not be like the hypocrites, for they love to pray standing in the synagogues and on the street corners to be seen by others. Truly I tell you, they have received their reward in full. ⁶ But when you pray, go into your room, close the door and pray to your Father, who is unseen. Then your Father, who sees what is done in secret, will reward you. ⁷ And when you pray, do not keep on babbling like pagans, for they think they will be heard because of their many words. ⁸ Do not be like them, for your Father knows what you need before you ask him.*

Intercessors ought to be like the Air Marshalls who ride on planes. They don't need to make their presence known unless there is a problem. And if they must make their presence known, you had better believe that somebody is either going to jail or somebody is going to die. Like these hidden officers of the law, true intercessors don't seek the limelight because they understand, by nature, that what they do in the realm of the spirit is a secret thing between them and their King. They are less impressed with you calling them an intercessor and more excited about the work of intercession. They don't have to have titles, or business cards. They are undercover operators for the Kingdom. Their greatest pleasure in life is communicating with God. They act and behave like Nehemiah. Nehemiah's not leaky. He's not running around town telling everybody what God is showing him. He didn't tell the government, he didn't tell the church leadership, he didn't post it on Facebook. He quietly makes a careful inspection of his coast. Then he is strategic about how and when the data he has gathered should be released.

Why do we need to do it Nehemiah's way? Because snitches get stitches. While you're busy running around town sharing everything that God has showed you, trying to appear 'deep', the enemy is launching a counter attack based on the information that is coming out of your mouth. Let me tell you something else about leaky people. God treats leaky people the same way that you and I do. When you have people in your life that tell everything, you only tell them what everybody else already knows. Shhh, the role of the intercessor is to be quiet and inspect the land. The enemy can't read your mind. Don't set yourself up for unnecessary backlash and retaliation.

# Role # 4 The Role of the Intercessor is to:

# BE PROPERLY SET IN YOUR WARD

## Isaiah 62: 1

*[1] For Zion's sake I will not keep silent, for Jerusalem's sake I will not remain quiet, till her vindication shines out like the dawn, her salvation like a blazing torch.*

## Isaiah 62:6-7

*I have posted watchmen on your walls, Jerusalem; they will never be silent day or night. You who call on the LORD, give yourselves no rest, [7] and give him no rest till he establishes Jerusalem and makes her the praise of the earth.*

## Isaiah 21:6-8

*For thus has the Lord said to me: "Go, set a watchman, Let him declare what he sees."[7] And he saw a chariot with a pair of horsemen, A chariot of donkeys, and a chariot of camels, And he listened earnestly with great care.[8] Then he cried, "A lion my Lord! I stand continually on the watchtower in the daytime; I have sat at my post every night.*

Isaiah 62 reads, "I have posted watchmen on your walls, Jerusalem," but that could very well read: "I have posted watchmen on the walls of America." Or the walls of the school district, or the white house, or whatever else you want to name. God places watchmen on different walls. He causes them to sound the alarm about different things. In both the secular arena and the church arena. You may be wired or bent to pray for certain things. Understand that your wiring is your wiring. Not necessarily your neighbor's wiring. Your neighbor may be bent a different way. It's not wrong, it's just different. So stop getting angry at people, when they don't see what you see. Being properly set in your ward is you, as the intercessor, owning the responsibility to sound the alarm concerning the thing that God gave you.

It is important that the intercessor be properly set in their ward. Think of the ward as the geographical, spherical, and spiritual realm of influence that God has given them to *shamar*- hedge about as with thorns or protect. When intercessors get set in their rightful positions- their wards, their job is to cry aloud and spare not. That means hold nothing back. So many times in prayer people find themselves holding back. I always set aside time for talk back whenever I lead corporate prayer. You ask the people during the talk back did they press that burden all the way through. They'll tell you honestly, "No, I didn't go all the way in. I could have gone further but I found myself holding back."

Well here's the problem with that folks: we don't just kind of eat, we don't kind of make love, we keep going until we get our fill, or we reach breakthrough. Here's another point I want to make about being properly set in your ward. Sometimes the people of God treat intercessors like they are spiritual dump sites. Can you pray for this? Can you pray for that? Can you? If you're not careful you'll never be able to attack the things in the spirit realm God wants you to go after. And the people of God will prayer pimp you.

One day I got a text from someone on my way to $4^{th}$ Watch, the 3-6 AM prayer meeting I conduct at my home church, every Friday morning. The text message read: Minister Catrina my mom just was diagnosed with stage 4 cancer can you pray for her at the $4^{th}$ watch this morning? Thanks, love ya. Have a good time at the watch. Yawning emoji. *Really?* I may have compassion for your mother, but don't you love your mother? Aren't you desperate enough for her healing that you will rise early and seek God's face for her and cry out for her healing? Because the truth of the matter is I may pray for her, but the Lord may not give me the burden to lay on that topic and stay on it. I promise you, nobody can press in the realm of the spirit for your mama the way you can.

Now of course, as an intercessor, I will lift up the peoples' prayer requests, but I focus most of my prayer energy on the issues that affect my own ward. That may sound cold to you, but look around at the condition of the body of Christ. There is so much work we all must rebuild the wall. I don't have time to build my area of the wall and your area of the wall too. And if you think that someone else's prayers over the things that God has given you hold more weight and sway in God's eyes then yours do . . .well, then, you don't understand prayer and how the spirit realm works. If you previously thought that way, that's okay, that's why you are reading this book, to get an understanding. And on that note, here's the principle I want you to take away from this section:

## PRINCIPLE #7

**WHEN GOD HAS APPOINTED TERRITORY TO YOU, NO ONE'S WORD HOLDS MORE SWAY IN THE COURTS OF HEAVEN THAN YOURS DOES.**

The role of the intercessor is to be properly set in his or her ward.

## Role #5: The Role of the Intercessor is to:

## APPROACH HEAVEN WITH THE RIGHT POSITION AND POSTURE

## Matthew 9: 18-19, 23-25

*While he was saying this, a synagogue leader came and knelt before him and said, "My daughter has just died. But come and put your hand on her, and she will live." 19Jesus got up and went with him, and so did his disciples. 23When Jesus entered the synagogue leader's house and saw the noisy crowd and people playing pipes, 24he said, **"Go away. The girl is not dead but asleep."** But they laughed at him. 25After the crowd had been put outside, he went in and took the girl by the hand, and she got up.*

## Luke 11:5-8

*Then Jesus said to them, "Suppose you have a friend, and you go to him at midnight and say, 'Friend, lend me three loaves of bread; ⁶ a friend of mine on a journey has come to me, and I have no food to offer him.' ⁷ And suppose the one inside answers, 'Don't bother me. The door is already locked, and my children and I are in bed. I can't get up and give you anything.' ⁸ I tell you, even though he will not get up and give you the bread because of friendship, yet because of your shameless audacity he will surely get up and give you as much as you need.*

Intercessors must be tuned to God's broadcast station. We have to see the thing the way God sees it. The child is not dead, she's asleep. That's how you bring Heaven into Earth. You have to know the mind of Heaven. In the Luke 11 passage, The disciples had just said to Jesus, "John taught his disciples how to pray, will you teach us how to pray?" So Jesus responds by telling them this story, so that they might know how to approach the King of Glory in His position as the Judge of the Whole Earth. Remember, this is the God Abraham was talking to when he asked the question, "Won't the Judge of the Whole Earth do right? Abe is God's friend, for sure, but please understand that when Abe is standing in the gap for Sodom and Gomorrah he is not standing before the same Jesus who was eating a turkey sandwich at his house a few moments ago. This is God in His official capacity. This is the Judge of the Whole Earth. He's perfectly just. And He won't just hear your request because you have a personal relationship with Him. When you stand in the gap you had better be coming with something more than your personal relationship with Him. You must be bold and audacious enough to ask because when He holds out that scepter to you He's not your friend in that moment. He's the King of the Universe. The Maker of all things.

It took me a long time to grasp this concept. Because all I ever knew Him as, was my daddy, my Abba, My big brother Jesus, and Holy Ghost, my friend. He spoke to me for the first time in my life on my sixteenth birthday. He wooed me with His loving kindness and compassion. I didn't know Him as a Man of War, I didn't know Him as the Head of State. He was just . . . Daddy. So, when the enemy would pursue me I would run at breakneck speed. I would fly into His arms and He would counsel me. He was very patient with me. But after a while, I grew older,

I grew stronger and He required me to change my posture. Now let's talk about posture for a minute. Because you should talk to God one way and you should talk to devils another way. I do not believe one should ever do intentional warfare on their knees. Now, you may have begun on your knees and found that, all of a sudden, your prayer has shifted to warfare, but you can't start a war, a riot, or a rebellion on your knees.

One of the first things my Abba taught me when He was training my hands to war was to recognize the proper order of things. He has assigned the enemy a place under our feet. So that means when I talk to the devil, I can't be on my knees, I need to be on my feet. The job of the intercessor is to approach heaven with the right position and posture.

### Role # 6 The Role of the Intercessor is to:

## HARNESS THE EXPONENTIAL POWER OF GOD FOUND IN CORPORATE PRAYER

# Genesis 11:1-8

*Now the whole world had one language and a common speech. ² As people moved eastward, they found a plain in Shinar and settled there.³ They said to each other, "Come, let's make bricks and bake them thoroughly." They used brick instead of stone, and tar for mortar. ⁴ Then they said, "Come, let us build ourselves a city, with a tower that reaches to the heavens, so that we may make a name for ourselves; otherwise we will be scattered over the face of the whole earth."⁵ But the LORD came down to see the city and the tower the people were building. ⁶ The LORD said, "If as one people speaking the same language they have begun to do this, then nothing they plan to do will be impossible for them. ⁷ Come, let us go down and confuse their language so they will not understand each other."⁸ So the LORD scattered them from there over all the earth, and they stopped building the city.*

Now this is a negative passage, but here's the point I want you to catch. When the people were unified they could build. When God broke their unity, they could no longer build. The Lord, Himself, said that if these people are unified, there is nothing that will be impossible for them. This is the unredeemed man we are talking about. This is the godless, sin-sick man. What could the people of God do if they were in one accord?

# 1 Corinthians 1:10

*[10] I appeal to you, brothers by the name of our Lord Jesus Christ, that all of you agree, and that there be no divisions among you, but that you be united in the same mind and the same judgment.*

Another word for unity is agreement. You must be very careful what you put your agreement to. If we really understood the power of agreement, we would stop talking about the things that bother us and we would put them to prayer. You see talking on the matter creates an atmosphere of disunity. But if you simply remove your agreement from the situation you would have victory. The Lord spoke to me years ago and said very simply, "Catrina, some people's agreement means more than others." The apostles understood the power of agreement, so they pleaded with the people of God to grab hold of this powerful weapon every single chance they got.

Don't let denominations divide you, don't let affiliations divide you. Don't let gender, race, or ethnicity divide you. Don't let baptisms divide you, don't let tongues divide you. Don't let diet or music or belly buttons divide you. I won't worship with anybody who's got an outie belly button. The true worshipers, that worship Him in spirit and truth, all have inny belly buttons. The apostles said, "Listen folks, stop all this foolishness and let the supremacy of Jesus be the baseline." They sat under Jesus who taught them the value of unity. The very One who said that if a house is divided against itself it will not stand. And if Satan is divided against himself, his kingdom will not stand. What exactly is Jesus saying here? He's saying that you cannot run a successful revolution without unity. The people of God cannot exact judgment against the enemy without unity. Moses tells us in Leviticus 26 what can happen when just a few people of God come into unity:

## Leviticus 26: 7-8

*7You will pursue your enemies, and they will fall by the sword before you. 8Five of you will chase a hundred, and a hundred of you will chase ten thousand, and your enemies will fall by the sword before you.*

When the people of God come together, this crazy kind of math starts taking place. One puts a thousand to flight. Two people can route ten thousand, three 100 thousand. Deuteronomy 32:30 tells you why this is even possible:

## Deuteronomy 32:30

*How could one man chase a thousand, or two put ten thousand to flight, unless their Rock had sold them, unless the Lord had given them up?*

The Rock of Ages is against them and He's for you. So, if just two of you would join together in faith and unity He'll fight for you.

## Nehemiah 4:19

*[19] Then I said to the nobles, the officials and the rest of the people, "The work is extensive and spread out, and we are widely separated from each other along the wall. Whenever you hear the sound of the trumpet, join us there our God will fight for us.*

I would that you would catch two revelations from this passage. A call for corporate prayer and a call for city wide prayer. There should be times and seasons where the intercessors sound the alarm and call all the people into times of corporate prayer. You must call ALL the people into prayer. God's end-time plan is to teach everybody how to build. Just like Nehemiah mobilized all the people to build the wall. The role of the intercessor is to sound the alarm and call the people into corporate prayer.

You should be leading corporate prayer times that anyone in your congregation can come to. This is in order for the work, which is extensive, to be accomplished. Unite the people of God to come together and cry out. There should be times and seasons of gathering together just to tug on God's heart.

I also want you to read Nehemiah 4:19 and catch the revelation for city-wide corporate prayer or multi-church prayer. Nehemiah is talking to the intercessors who built the wall that surrounded the entire city. Nehemiah said we are all busy, we know that. The work is extensive. It's spread out. It's hard to remain unified given these conditions. But wherever you hear the sound of the trumpet blast, join us right there and our God will fight for us.

I've been doing this for a very long time now, and I am convinced that no one single church can effectively build and maintain the entire prayer wall that surrounds an entire city. You can only build your section of the wall. You might say well in my book that's good enough. But what happens when the enemy enters your home or your church because of the other unprotected parts?

Now, the unfortunate fact is, that every church will not build the wall of intercession. Not until the very end comes and the people of God become really desperate will all the people of God on the earth began to answer the call of prayer. But we don't need everybody to answer the call. We just need a few somebodies to do it. Because when the people of God come together in one accord the Lord does something for us. He gives us this crazy math we spoke about a few moments ago.

# Joel 2:2-11

*² A day of darkness and gloom, a day of clouds and blackness. Like dawn spreading across the mountains a large and mighty army comes, such as never was in ancient times nor ever will be in ages to come. ³ Before them fire devours, behind them a flame blazes. Before them the land is like the garden of Eden, behind them, a desert waste— nothing escapes them. ⁴ They have the appearance of horses; they gallop along like cavalry. ⁵ With a noise like that of chariots they leap over the mountaintops, like a crackling fire consuming stubble, like a mighty army drawn up for battle.*

*⁶ At the sight of them, nations are in anguish; every face turns pale. ⁷ They charge like warriors; they scale walls like soldiers. They all march in line, not swerving from their course. ⁸ They do not jostle each other; each marches straight ahead. They plunge through defenses without breaking ranks. ⁹ They rush upon the city; they run along the wall. They climb into the houses; like thieves they enter through the windows. ¹⁰ Before them the earth shakes, the heavens tremble, the sun and moon are darkened, and the stars no longer shine. ¹¹ The LORD thunders at the head of his army; his forces are beyond number and mighty is the army that obeys his command. The day of the LORD is great; it is dreadful. Who can endure it?*

We went over this passage in chapter four, where we learned that this is what corporate intercession looks like in the spirit realm when the people of God press. This army is unified and unstoppable. They sing and they dance before the Lord and they set people free. They are orderly, they all march together in a line. They know how to follow the leader. There is no pushing and shoving in the spirit realm, No one seeking the limelight and they all ascend as one. Together they are a lean mean fighting machine and the gates of hell can't stand against them.

## Acts 2: 1-4

*And when the day of Pentecost was fully come, they were all with one accord in one place. 2And suddenly there came a sound from heaven as of a rushing mighty wind, and it filled all the house where they were sitting. 3And there appeared unto them cloven tongues like as of fire, and it sat upon each of them. 4And they were all filled with the Holy Ghost, and began to speak with other tongues, as the Spirit gave them utterance.*

Please understand that I keep talking about unity because unity is to prayer what flour is to cake batter. Sometimes the rubble in our lives impedes unity. In other words, our flesh nature, and our sin nature keep us from unifying with one another. You call a prayer meeting at 5 o'clock, the spirit of disunity is the first one there. You run in the door at five after five, he showed up at 4:15. He's got his church clothes on and a great big old Bible in his hand. He is

Christianity without the Cross, and his next of kin is Religion. This devil comes to prayer and he's judging everything that's happening in the prayer meeting. "Why her tongues sound like that? Why they got to pray so loud? Who died and left them in charge?" His assignment from the pit of hell is to destroy the unity. He knows the Word better than you or I. He has studied the scripture that says if any two on earth touch and agree it will be done by my Father in heaven. And he can't have that because if the people of God get to this place called unity, if they all arrive at the same place and they get on one accord, another Pentecost episode will break out and the Holy Ghost will show up with them daggone tongues of fire and burn his kingdom down.

## Proverbs 24: 7

*7 Wisdom is too high for fools; in the assembly at the gate they must not open their mouths.*

This is another one of those 24/7s I spoke to you about earlier. I like this verse because it gives us instructions on how wise people are to conduct themselves in a corporate gathering. This is the twin verse to Psalm 24:7 that tells us to lift up our heads o ye gates and the king of glory shall come in. Like its twin, its position in the scripture tells us how often we are supposed to do this, 24/7. All the time.

Wherever the people of God gather, there is a gate or spiritual portal that opens in the earth. It's the place where deals are made. It's the place where laws are enforced and created. It's a place of power and transaction. Laws can be overturned at the gate. Death can be stayed at the gate. Prisoners can be exonerated— fully pardoned and released at the gate. You can route things that would take you years to conquer alone, and thousands of dollars in therapy bills, quickly at the gate. I've seen it happen. It's happened for me. There is true transformational power that happens at the gate.

I know of no other ministry that can truly transform a person, like meeting God at the gates. Having a *Paga (a life altering encounter)* experience. I can preach to you till the cows come home. I can teach your socks off, but when you have an encounter with the King of Glory for yourself at the gates, He will change you into another man. Notice the scripture in Ps 24/7 didn't say the Lamb of God, The Prince of Peace comes through this gate. It says the King of Glory comes through this gate. That lets you know He's coming in His official judicial capacity. This is the Judge of the Whole Earth, the same One that Abraham bartered with for Sodom and Gomorrah. This is the same One that Moses bartered with for the people of Israel.

Yet, nevertheless, Proverbs 24:7 says it's always going to be at least one idiot in the room. All of this is going on in the realm of the spirit. Everybody else is crying out before the King and the fool is sitting there like a lump on the wall not saying nothing. Everybody else here's the wind of the spirit. They hear elevator music. I beseech you my brother, my sister, (that's King James speak for beg.) When the King of Glory shows up in your prayer gathering, please, I beg you don't be a fool.

## Role # 7 The Role of the Intercessor is to:

## REMOVE & RECOVER

## Nehemiah 4:10

*Meanwhile, the people in Judah said, "The strength of the laborers is giving out, and there is so much rubble that we cannot rebuild the wall."*

The role of the intercessor is to go up in the spirit realm and remove the spiritual rubble, first in their own life, then in the institution they are praying for. So that the house can be prepared for the Day of Judgment. What is spiritual rubble? It's weights, woundedness, demons. It's unforgiveness. The things we need to be delivered from. Every person has them, every ministry has them, every government and institution has them. Devils. We all got devils. True building cannot happen until all of the rubble, the debris is moved out of the way. The job of the intercessor is to clear away spiritual rubble. This happens naturally in prayer. As you press in the realm of the spirit, sometimes you may feel sick. You may feel like you have to vomit or that your bowels want to move. You may feel like passing gas. For the sake of the other people who are sitting around the prayer circle, most people will try to hold that in. Don't. Those are the weights falling off. Deliverance is a by- product of the press.

## Luke 10:19

*19 I have given you authority to trample on snakes and scorpions and to overcome all the power of the enemy; nothing will harm you.*

## Psalm 18: 44-45

*44foreigners cower before me; as soon as they hear of me, they obey me.45They all lose heart; they come trembling from their strongholds.*

## Mark 9:17-18

*17 A man in the crowd answered, "Teacher, I brought you my son, who is possessed by a spirit that has robbed him of speech. 18 Whenever it seizes him, it throws him to the ground. He foams at the mouth, gnashes his teeth and becomes rigid. I asked your disciples to drive out the spirit, but they could not."*

Once you've gotten a certain amount of deliverance for yourself, you will be able to drive out demons. The role of the intercessor is to build up enough muscle to be able to drive them out. How do we build muscle in the spirit? We built our spiritual muscles when we press, especially in our heavenly language.

## Isaiah 58:12

*[12] Your people will rebuild the ancient ruins and will raise up the age-old foundations; you will be called Repairer of Broken Walls, Restorer of Streets with Dwellings.*

The role of the intercessor is to rekindle old moves of God, and to recover lost mantles. Go back and pick up your grandmother's mantle. We often talk about the sins of the forefathers being visited upon the children, but what about the blessings? Some of those blessings are waiting, sitting in heavenly accounts, for someone to tap into. This is the kinsman redeemer/ blood avenger's role because sometimes, actually, oftentimes you will have to fight to regain those mantles.

Some of you may remember the famous commercial General Motors put out in the 80's. "This is not your father's oldsmobile. This is a new generation of olds." It's a great slogan, it implies that what they are doing is new, but that it's steeped in legacy. I often tell people when I minister deliverance that if you want something different from God, you must be willing to go a different way.

## Matthew 18:21-22

*Then Peter came to Jesus and asked, "Lord, how many times shall I forgive my brother or sister who sins against me? Up to seven times?" 22Jesus answered, "I tell you, not seven times, but seventy-seven times.*

## Matthew 5: 21-26

*You have heard that it was said to the people long ago, 'You shall not murder, and anyone who murders will be subject to judgment.' 22But I tell you that anyone who is angry with a brother or sister will be subject to judgment. Again, anyone who says to a brother or sister, 'Raca,' is answerable to the court. And anyone who says, 'You fool!' will be in danger of the fire of hell.23"Therefore, if you are offering your gift at the altar and there remember that your brother or sister has something against you, 24leave your gift there in front of the altar. First go and be reconciled to them; then come and offer your gift.25"Settle matters quickly with your adversary who is taking you to court. Do it while you are still together on the way, or your adversary may hand you over to the judge, and the judge may hand you over to the officer, and you may be thrown into prison.*

*26Truly I tell you, you will not get out until you have paid the last penny.*

Unforgiveness is some serious rubble. Matthew 5:23 says that if you are offering your gift before God and remember that your brother or sister has something against you to leave your gift and go and be reconciled. God will always bring offenses back to your mind. For the intercessor, unforgiveness is an absolute no no. Verse 25 tells you why: settle matters quickly with your adversary who is taking you to court.

Jesus is not talking about the brother or sister who has the ought with you in verse 23. Jesus is talking about The Adversary. Jesus is telling you something about the heavenlies. He says, look, if there is offense in your heart towards your brethren, the evil one is filing a motion against you in the courts of heaven.

Didn't I tell you that the devil knows the law better than you? What a low-down dirty dude that Satan is. He inspired the dispute in the first place. But he's going to haul you into court based on this matter. Jesus says settle this thing before it gets before the Judge and settle it quickly. **Because the Judge will hear the case and** He may turn you over to the officer and you may be put into prison. Unless somebody comes along with an anointing to break you up out of that joint, you won't leave that cell until you pay back every last dime.

Here you see God's government at work. This is God's invisible kingdom. Unforgiveness keeps many people in bondage. If you have unforgiveness in your heart, I can almost guarantee you that a demon lives there. Tear his house down. If you have unforgiveness in your heart you are in prison.

I've been in deliverance situations where healing couldn't come forth until the person forgave. If that's you today, I pray that you catch this revelation and be immediately set free. So, here is Catrina's recipe for unforgiveness, that causes a root of bitterness to grow. Make a decision in your heart to forgive. Not based on how you feel, but based on the information you now know. Then pray fervently for that person who has wronged or hurt you every single day. That's how you bust yourself up out of prison. The role of the intercessor is to climb up in the realm of the spirit: remove and recover.

## Role #8 The Role of the Intercessor is to:

## **BUILD**

## 1 Corinthians 3:9- 15

*⁹ For we are co-workers in God's service; you are God's field, God's building. ¹⁰ By the grace God has given me, I laid a foundation as a wise builder, and someone else is building on it. But each one should build with care. ¹¹ For no one can lay any foundation* *other than the one already laid, which is Jesus Christ. $^{12}$ If anyone builds on this foundation using gold, silver, costly stones, wood, hay or straw, $^{13}$ their work will be shown for what it is, because the Day will bring it to light. It will be revealed with fire, and the fire will test the quality of each person's work. $^{14}$ If what has been built survives, the builder will receive a reward. $^{15}$ If it is burned up, the builder will suffer loss but yet will be saved—even though only as one escaping through the flames.*

When I say the word build I'm talking about two different types of building. The first I'm going to talk about is a very basic level of building through the avenue of prayer. We've been using the book of Nehemiah as a metaphor during this entire course. The nugget I want you to take away from 1Corinthians 3:9 is this: A wise master builder builds with prayer. You cannot build anything except through prayer. Not a marriage, not a ministry, not a career, not a family, nada. You must build on a foundation of prayer.

Not praying over that which God has given you, is like making a purchase, without checking your bank account. Your job as an intercessor is to become a wise master builder. You can only build wisely if you become a keeper of God's Word. God gives blueprints in prayer. We are to be architects in the realm of the spirit. Become a keeper of God's Word, because He honors His Word above all else. A good **architect** keeps plans. Written plans. Become a chronicler of God's Word. How do you become a chronicler of God's Word? It's simple beloved, you write it down! The enemy will surely tell you that God isn't answering your prayers. Become a chronicler of the things He says to you concerning the territory He has given you.

That is why my book, *Doing Business with God*: *An Everyday Guide to Prayer and Journaling*, is included in the Intercession 101 course. So you can learn to practice this discipline of writing down your prayers and become a chronicler of God's Word.

## Haggai 1:7-8

*This is what the LORD Almighty says: "Give careful thought to your ways. ⁸ Go up into the mountains and bring down timber and build my house, so that I may take pleasure in it and be honored," says the LORD.*
⁹

## Isaiah 57:14

*And it will be said: "Build up, build up, prepare the road! Remove the obstacles out of the way of my people."*

The second type of building I am talking about is the building of a platform in the spirit that happens in corporate prayer. Let's say we are in a corporate prayer setting. One person is praying. What should the other people around the circle be doing? Thinking about their grocery list? No, their job is to build. The person leading the prayer starts off praying by faith. As they began to press, to reach unto, the Spirit of God begins to pray through them. The people of God have to build a platform underneath them so that the person can pull the prayers out of the realm of the spirit that God really wants prayed. These are the mechanics of prayer. Everybody doesn't need to know and understand this part, but the intercessors and the leaders in the house—them who are in-charge of the building process, certainly ought to.

Corporate prayer often falls flat when the people of God don't properly build a platform. You build a platform with your agreement. You build it with your "yes." You build it with your "Amen," and you build with your prayer language.

An intercessor must be a multitasker in the spirit. In other words, I have to be able to tune my ear to the prayer coming out the person's mouth who is at the time leading the charge. I have to pray in tongues at the same time, but I cannot pray in such a way that I overpower the one leading the prayer. I also have to tune my ear to the shifts. The role of the intercessor is to go up in the realm of the spirit and build.

## Role #9 The role of the intercessor is to:

## **BRING GOD'S GOVERNMENT INTO THE EARTH**

## 1Timothy 2:1-7

*I urge, then, first of all, that petitions, prayers, intercession and thanksgiving be made for all people— 2for kings and all those in authority, that we may live peaceful and quiet lives in all godliness and holiness. 3This is good, and pleases God our Savior, 4who wants all people to be saved and to come to a knowledge of the truth. 5For there is one God and one mediator between God and mankind, the man Christ Jesus, 6who gave himself as a ransom for all people. This has now been witnessed to at the proper time. 7And for this purpose I was appointed a herald and an apostle—I am telling the truth, I am not lying—and a true and faithful teacher of the Gentiles.*


## Matthew 9:35-38

*Jesus went through all the towns and villages, teaching in their synagogues, proclaiming the good news of the kingdom and healing every disease and sickness. 36When he saw the crowds, he had compassion on them, because they were harassed and helpless, like sheep without a shepherd. 37Then he said to his disciples, "The harvest is plentiful but the workers are few. 38Ask the Lord of the harvest, therefore, to send out workers into his harvest field."*

Jesus said pray to the Lord of the Harvest to send the laborers. He didn't say pray to the Lion of Judah, or El Shaddai, the multi-breasted one. He said tug on heaven with the knowledge that God wants all people to be saved. Tug on heaven's door with the knowledge that there is only one way into the kingdom. Pray for conversion. When you pray to the Lord of the Harvest to send the laborers, you are praying for revolution to enter the land. And the purpose of a revolution is to free the people from an unjust governmental system.

1 Timothy is also important because it tells us to pray for good earthly government. This is very important. This passage tells us that when the people of God pray for the city they can live peaceful and quiet lives. Could it be that in war torn places there is not enough intercession being lifted up? "That we may live peaceful and quiet lives." I want you to understand that this is not governmental intercession. We're going to talk about that in the next section. This is simply praying for good government, right here on earth. 1 Timothy tells us in the above passage that if we don't have good government, if we don't have peace in our streets, then people of God aren't praying into that area enough.

The role of the intercessor is to be involved with the political affairs of our society. The seat of government is in the church. But most of us won't take this position. Most of us are like Whoopi Goldberg's character in the movie, *The Color Purple*. Remember Ceily? Remember Ceily gave her stepson, Harpo, some bad advice. She told him to beat his wife, Sophia. When Sophia confronted Ceily, who had been battered by her own husband Mister, do you remember her response? She told Sophia, "This world won't last long, heaven be on the other side." Sophia's response to her was. "You better bash Mister in the head now and think about heaven later."

People of God, you better take the devil to task now and think about heaven later. Get involved with the political conversation happening in your city. CAST YOUR VOTE IN THE SPRIRT REALM AND IN THE NATURAL REALM. The seat of government is in the church. Stop playing spiritual roulette at the polls. Holy Ghost tell me which candidate to pick. You are a ruler and you are a gate, Do your research on the people running for office. Don't you know beloved, that we will judge angels? Certainly, we can judge between to political opponents. **Not voting is a sign of the church being too self-absorbed.**

## Jeremiah 5:1-2

*"Go up and down the streets of Jerusalem, look around and consider, search through her squares. If you can find but one person who deals honestly and seeks the truth, I will forgive this city. ² Although they say, 'As surely as the LORD lives,' still they are swearing falsely."*

God is concerned about cities. God is concerned about how people conduct themselves in cities. He is concerned about truth and justice. He holds cities accountable for wicked activity, that's why we need intercessors. It is the job of the intercessor to pray for good government. It is the role of the intercessor to cry out for the spiritual climate of their city. The role of the intercessor is to bring God's government into the earth.

## Role #10 The role of the intercessor is:

## TO PROPERLY DIS-BAND THE BURDEN

## Lamentations 3:48-51

*$^{48}$ Streams of tears flow from my eyes because my people are destroyed. $^{49}$ My eyes will flow unceasingly, without relief, $^{50}$ until the LORD looks down from heaven and sees. $^{51}$ What I see brings grief to my soul because of all the women of my city.*

## Isaiah 21:1-4

*A prophecy against the Desert by the Sea: Like whirlwinds sweeping through the southland, an invader comes from the desert, from a land of terror. 2A dire vision has been shown to me: The traitor betrays, the looter takes loot. Elam, attack! Media, lay siege! I will bring to an end all the groaning she caused. 3At this my body is racked with pain, pangs seize me, like those of a woman in labor; I am staggered by what I hear, I am bewildered by what I see. 4My heart falters, fear makes me tremble; the twilight I longed for has become a horror to me.*

The last role of the intercessor is one of the most important ones, but also one of the most overlooked ones. The role of the intercessor is to disband the burden. The Lord gives me some amazing gifts every year for my birthday. One year He gave me this particular revelation. He said, the enemy has calculated the time in the earth that he has to put up with you because you have not yet learned how to properly disband the burden.

I don't find that I have to teach intercessors how to carry the burden. Carrying the burden is easy for those who have a heart for prayer. But what I do have to teach them is how to properly get rid of it. You see the burden, though it is spiritual in nature, sits on our natural bodies. That's why Isaiah is feeling pains like a woman in labor in the above passage as a result of the vision he is seeing. It is also why the writer of Lamentations (most likely the Prophet Jeremiah) is crying. Prophets are particularly susceptible to this issue by the way. Jeremiah was known as the weeping prophet. He cried about everything. He said he could hear the sound of the horses and chariots coming to carry the people off into captivity. In order to understand why this is so, you have to understand the call and appointment that was on Jeremiah's life. He was sent to a people on their way into captivity. A people who would not hear him. God told Jeremiah, "Look don't go to any weddings and don't go to any funerals. Do not celebrate or mourn these people because I'm done with them." At one point God even tells Jeremiah, "Don't even pray for them anymore because the judgment against them is sealed." That is an awful place for an intercessor to be in. Jeremiah wept, that's how he dis-banded the burden.

Some intercessors are like Jeremiah, they cry all the time and then they get mad at themselves for crying all the time. But tears can help you to properly disband the burden. Physical exercise can also help you to disband the burden. If you do not properly give the burden over to God, you can find yourself over eating, or vegging out in front of the television. You can find yourself every now and then just simply checking out of life, because the prayer burden becomes mentally and emotionally oppressive to you. In the meantime, the burden is hiding out in your fat cells, and sitting on your muscles, it's sitting on your lungs, your heart, your liver and your spleen, cutting away at your life. As intercessors, we are meant to pray the burden through. We are not meant to become pack animals in the spirit realm.

So this is how you properly disband the burden: you pray it through the moment it's dropped into your spirit. You pray until you have relief. You don't override the feeling that tells you it's still there, you pray until it completely lifts, and you have relief.

†

# CHAPTER EIGHT
# GOVERMENTAL INTERCESSION

When you enter into the realm of governmental intercession you wage war against an enemy who has brought a legal claim against you in the courts of heaven and assured that your destruction is legislated. He's got a right to come against you or the thing, the people group, the nation you are praying for. When we talk about governmental intercession we are talking about waging war against structures and systems of operation. Principalities and Powers. This isn't ground level warfare anymore. These aren't ground level troops. These aren't demons and imps these are principalities. Let's take a look at the first two passages, Esther 3:8-11, and Exodus 1.

## Esther 3:8-11

*⁸ Then Haman said to King Xerxes, "There is a certain people dispersed among the peoples in all the provinces of your kingdom who keep themselves separate. Their customs are different from those of all other people, and they do not obey the king's laws; it is not in the king's best interest to tolerate them. ⁹ If it pleases the king, let a decree be issued to destroy them, and I will give ten thousand talents[ of silver to the king's administrators for the royal treasury."[10] So the king took his signet ring from his finger and gave it to Haman son of Hammedatha, the Agagite, the enemy of the Jews. [11] "Keep the money," the king said to Haman, "and do with the people as you please."*

## Exodus 1: 6-17

*Now Joseph and all his brothers and all that generation died, 7but the Israelites were exceedingly fruitful; they multiplied greatly, increased in numbers and became so numerous that the land was filled with them.8Then a new king, to whom Joseph meant nothing, came to power in Egypt. 9"Look," he said to his people, "the Israelites have become far too numerous for us. 10Come, we must deal shrewdly with them or they will become even more numerous and, if war breaks out, will join our enemies, fight against us and leave the country."11So they put slave masters over them to oppress them with forced labor, and they built Pithom and Rameses as store cities for Pharaoh. 12But the more they were oppressed, the more they multiplied and spread; so the Egyptians came to dread the Israelites 13and worked them ruthlessly. 14They made their lives bitter with harsh labor in brick and mortar and with all kinds of work in the fields; in all their harsh labor the Egyptians worked them ruthlessly.15The king of Egypt said to the Hebrew midwives, whose names were Shiphrah and Puah, 16"When you are helping the Hebrew women during childbirth on the delivery stool, if you see that the baby is a boy, kill him; but if it is a girl, let her live." 17The midwives, however, feared God and did not do what the king of Egypt had told them to do; they let the boys live.*

The battle in Esther started long before Haman hated the Jews. Haman is just an embodiment of the principality that tried to snuff the Israelites out in Egypt. It's the same principality that operated in and through the demi-god pharaoh, who legislated the destruction of millions of little boys during Moses's time. It's the same principality that operated again through King Herod, to mass murder millions of little boys during Jesus's time. This principality has read the Word. He knows the Word of God better than you or I. He knew that in Jesus's generation a deliverer was coming and in Moses's generation a deliverer was coming, so he made certain to legalize their demise.

Here's the thing I want you to understand, God isn't unaware of what's going on. Sometimes I hear people saying things like, well where is God in all of this? Doesn't He know? Doesn't He understand? Of course He does, beloved. It was His signet ring that sealed the document and made it law.

Why would the lover of my soul and your soul do something like that? Because He is also the Judge of the Whole Earth. He is perfectly righteous. And when Satan comes before His throne room with a legitimate petition and there is no intercessor to stand in the gap, He must grant his request.

Satan prays did you know that? Much more than the people of God. That's why I believe that the Lord has called me and set me on the wall to do this work. Because the water level of intercession in the church is too low. The midwives practiced governmental intercession. Esther and Mordecai practiced governmental intercession. Moses's mother and sister both practiced governmental intercession. Daniel also practiced governmental intercession, as did Shadrach, Meshach and Abendnego—they all practiced governmental intercession. But the real question is, will you? Because this same principality who killed the people of God back then is still operating in the earth now. He has territorial holdings over your nation and your city. He's looking for the next generation of deliverers. I call them the New Breed. And there are not enough mid-wives on the wall. Not enough Miriams on the wall. You might ask, how did they do it? How did they practice governmental intercession? The moment they realized that God's kingdom was greater than any other kingdom, that His government superseded any other government, they were catapulted into the realm of governmental intercession.

## Psalm 24:1-2

*[1] The earth is the LORD's, and everything in it,*
*the world, and all who live in it;*

*² for he founded it on the seas*
  *and established it on the waters.*

## Colossians: 1:15-18

*15The Son is the image of the invisible God, the firstborn over all creation. 16For in him all things were created: things in heaven and on earth, visible and invisible, whether thrones or powers or rulers or authorities; all things have been created through him and for him. 17He is before all things, and in him all things hold together. 18And he is the head of the body, the church; he is the beginning and the firstborn from among the dead, so that in everything he might have the supremacy.*

In the above Psalm passage and the Colossians passage we learn that God alone holds all territorial rights. We can't even talk about governmental intercession without understanding this. Colossians tells us that everything was made by Him and for Him. All things visible and all things invisible. Thrones, powers, rulers, authorities—this is a breakdown of the angelic kingdom both good and bad. This verse says they all work for Him who is the image of the Invisible God. Now these very words: thrones, powers, rulers, authorities, implies that these angelic entities have been given territory. By territory I mean a sphere of influence whereby they are allowed to operate in.

So, if the first rule of governmental intercession is to understand that God owns all authority, the second rule of governmental intercession is to understand that God can, will, and does give territory to whomever He pleases. Let me remind you that it was God who sent the demon to torment and discipline on record two kings: Saul and Nebuchadnezzar.

## Deuteronomy 32: 7-9

*Remember the days of old; consider the generations long past. Ask your father and he will tell you, your elders, and they will explain to you. 8When the Most High gave the nations their inheritance, when he divided all mankind, he set up boundaries for the peoples according to the number of the sons of Israel. 9For the Lord's portion is his people, Jacob his allotted inheritance.*

If you understand the first and second rules— that God owns all authority and He gives it to whomever He pleases—it will go well with you. You will operate with decorum and decency in the realm of the spirit and you will have success in the spirit realm when you go up to fight.

## Psalms 23: 10-11

*Do not move an ancient boundary stone or encroach on the fields of the fatherless, 11for their Defender is strong; he will take up their case against you.*

## Proverbs 22:28

*Don't cheat your neighbor by moving the ancient boundary markers set up by previous generations.*

## Deuteronomy 27:17

*Cursed is anyone who moves their neighbor's boundary stone." Then all the people shall say, "Amen!"*

Territory is a really big deal in the realm of the spirit. That's why intercessors should not go around pulling things down willy-nilly in the spirit realm. Many of these boundary lines have been put in place long before you got here, your ancestors fully participated and were in agreement with the reigning demonic forces installed and unless God gives you the green light and the wherewithal to attack them, they will be here long after you leave. I've heard of intercessors doing ridiculous things like renting helicopters to go up Mount Everest and pull down the Queen of

Heaven. This is absolute foolishness. When you are messing around with the little boys, you might just get your clothes beat off you. But when you are messing with the big boys, this type of stupidity can get you killed. When you encroach illegally in the spirit realm upon a principality's field, you commit the crime of 2 Peter 1, you slander angels.

## 2 Peter 1:3, 9-12

*But there were also false prophets among the people, just as there will be false teachers among you. They will secretly introduce destructive heresies, even denying the sovereign Lord who bought them—bringing swift destruction on themselves. 2Many will follow their depraved conduct and will bring the way of truth into disrepute. 3In their greed these teachers will exploit you with fabricated stories. Their condemnation has long been hanging over them, and their destruction has not been sleeping. 9if this is so, then the Lord knows how to rescue the godly from trials and to hold the unrighteous for punishment on the day of judgment. 10This is especially true of those who follow the corrupt desire of the flesh and despise authority. Bold and arrogant, they are not afraid to heap abuse on celestial beings; 11yet even angels, although they are stronger and more powerful, do not heap abuse on such beings when bringing judgment on them from the Lord. 12But these people blaspheme in matters they do not understand. They are like unreasoning animals, creatures of instinct, born only to be caught and destroyed, and like animals they too will perish.*

The writer is saying this is pure foolishness. When angels are exacting God's ordained judgment—they don't even behave this way. People ought not behave this way either. The God of the whole earth is perfectly just. So let me go ahead and give you principle number eight:

## PRINCIPLE #8:

**AUTHORITY IN THE SPIRIT REALM IS REGULATED TO THE BOUNDARY LINES OF YOUR COAST. YOU WILL ONLY HAVE SUCCESS IN GOVERNMENTAL INTERCESSION WHEN YOU REMAIN WITHIN THE PARAMETERS OF YOUR ASSIGNED COAST.**

## Leviticus 26:6

*I will grant peace in the land, and you will lie down and no one will make you afraid. I will remove wild beasts from the land, and the sword will not pass through your country.*

## Psalm 16: 5-8

*Lord, you alone are my portion and my cup; you make my lot secure. 6The boundary lines have fallen for me in pleasant places; surely I have a delightful inheritance.7 I will praise the Lord, who counsels me; even at night my heart instructs me.8I keep my eyes always on the Lord. With him at my right hand, I will not be shaken.*


When you operate within the boundary lines of your authority, God makes your lot secure. No one will be able to make you afraid in your territory. You'll be able to cast out demons effortlessly. If someone tries to encroach upon your field, God Himself will fight against them. God will reveal the intruders to you during the night. As you sleep on your bed He will instruct you in your dreams how to deal with them that seek to poach and steal from you. Whenever I take new territory in the realm of the spirit I always have demonic visitations. These visitors always come to me in the form of a dream. God always shows me how to deal with them as He instructs my heart in the night (Psalm 16:7).


## Esther 8: 1-8

*8 That same day King Xerxes gave Queen Esther the estate of Haman, the enemy of the Jews. And Mordecai came into the presence of the king, for Esther had told how he was related to her. [2] The king* *took off his signet ring, which he had reclaimed from Haman, and presented it to Mordecai. And Esther appointed him over Haman's estate.³ Esther again pleaded with the king, falling at his feet and weeping. She begged him to put an end to the evil plan of Haman the Agagite, which he had devised against the Jews. ⁴ Then the king extended the gold scepter to Esther and she arose and stood before him.⁵ "If it pleases the king," she said, "and if he regards me with favor and thinks it the right thing to do, and if he is pleased with me, let an order be written overruling the dispatches that Haman son of Hammedatha, the Agagite, devised and wrote to destroy the Jews in all the king's provinces. ⁶ For how can I bear to see disaster fall on my people? How can I bear to see the destruction of my family?"⁷ King Xerxes replied to Queen Esther and to Mordecai the Jew, "Because Haman attacked the Jews, I have given his estate to Esther, and they have impaled him on the pole he set up. ⁸ **Now write another decree in the king's name** in behalf of the Jews as seems best to you, **and seal it with the king's signet ring**—for no document written in the king's name and sealed with his ring can be revoked."*

We all know the story of Esther and how she saved her people. If you don't know it. I encourage you to read about it in the book of Esther. It's a short book just ten chapters. But the entire book is all about governmental intercession. I want you to see that when the king takes off his ring and hands it to Mordecai he tells him to write a decree. Go ahead and say that with me. Write a decree. After he had him write the decree then the next thing he has him to do is to declare it. Now say that with me, Declare the decree! When the law (decree) is declared it's established. Notice the king did not tell Mordecai what law to write, he said write the decree that seems best to you.

There is a realm in the spirit where we don't pray we say. God takes off His signet ring and hands it to us in the spirit realm and we exact laws and write checks in His name.

## Haggai 2:20-23

*20 The word of the LORD came to Haggai a second time on the twenty-fourth day of the month: 21 "Tell Zerubbabel governor of Judah that I am going to shake the heavens and the earth. 22 I will overturn royal thrones and shatter the power of the foreign kingdoms. I will overthrow chariots and their drivers; horses and their riders will fall, each by the sword of his brother. 23 "'On that day,' declares the LORD Almighty, 'I will take you, my servant Zerubbabel son of Shealtiel,' declares the LORD, 'and I will make you like my signet ring, for I have chosen you,' declares the LORD Almighty."*

In governmental intercession you pray signet ring prayers. In governmental intercession you don't ask God to do what He has already equipped you to do. In other words, you don't ask Him to bind, to loose, to set free. You bind. You loose. You set free.

# The Role of the Prophet in Governmental Intercession

We cannot talk about governmental intercession without talking about the role of the prophet in intercession. We won't get into all the things that prophets do, because that's not the nature of this study. If you are interested in learning more about the prophetic office, please see my book entitled, *Divine Revelation for a Twitter Generation: Growing in the Prophetic.* As it relates to our study today, when I talk about the prophet I will try to stay within the realm of intercession.

## Hosea 12:13

*13And by a prophet the LORD brought Israel out of Egypt, and by a prophet was he preserved.*

Prophets are essential to governmental intercession because of their innate ability to declare and because of the otherworldly nature of the prophetic promise. Every true prophetic promise originates in the mind of God. That makes it otherworldly. It's superman. The prophetic promise is not bound by time because it's been spoken outside of time. It's not bound by the laws of physics, it's not bound by human customs or tradition. It has everything it needs to fulfill itself. Everything but one crucial ingredient. Agreement. When you are prophetic, not merely in name but in deed, your words carry spiritual weight. When you speak, angelic legions are dispatched & trucks start to move in the spirit realm because Heaven backs your word.

The Hosea passage speaks about two particular graces that should always accompany the prophetic minister. Did you hear me? I said *should*. The psalmist, David wrote in the 23$^{rd}$ Psalm that goodness and mercy followed him all the days of his life. Well prophets can say that deliverance and preservation follow them all the days of their life. In the realm of prayer these particular graces are extremely important.

Prophets in proper alignment keep ministries from falling apart, marriages from breaking up, they stay death at the gate. They encourage and strengthen the people of God and they vex troublemakers. They emit an aroma in the spirit realm that vexes people who slip into the body of Christ to do it harm, it makes them jittery, unwelcomed, and after a while it causes them to just up and leave. Prophets do this naturally and effortlessly just by virtue of their mantles.

Being a prophet is so much more than standing up in front of a group of people and saying thus said the Lord. In fact, giving a prophetic word is the least of what prophets are really called to do. I liken giving a prophetic word to that other duties as assigned by the supervisor category on your position description. Prophets in a house should always be participants in the prayer ministry. In fact, prayer ministries benefit when prophets oversee them. Prophets, when properly trained, have the ability to understand the innerworkings of prayer. Since prayer is communication with God, and since prophets specialize in studying the communication patterns of God, they ought to also specialize in prayer ministry.

## 2 Samuel 5:17-19

*When the Philistines heard that David had been anointed king over Israel, they went up in full force to search for him, but David heard about it and went down to the stronghold. 18Now the Philistines had come and spread out in the Valley of Rephaim; 19so David inquired of the Lord, "Shall I go and attack the Philistines? Will you deliver them into my hands?" The Lord answered him, "Go, for I will surely deliver the Philistines into your hands."*

## 2 Samuel 5:22-25

*Once more the Philistines came up and spread out in the Valley of Rephaim; 23so David inquired of the Lord, and he answered, "Do not go straight up, but circle around behind them and attack them in front of the poplar trees. 24As soon as you hear the sound of marching in the tops of the poplar trees, move quickly, because that will mean the Lord has gone out in front of you to strike the Philistine army." 25So David did as the Lord commanded him, and he struck down the Philistines all the way from Gibeon to Gezer.*

## Jeremiah 9:17-21

*Thus says the LORD of hosts, Consider you, and call for the mourning women, that they may come; and send for skillful women, that they may come:18And let them make haste, and take up a wailing for us, that our eyes may run down with tears, and our eyelids gush out with water.19For a voice of wailing is heard out of Zion, How are we plundered! we are greatly ashamed, because we have forsaken the land, because our dwellings have cast us out. 20Yet hear the word of the LORD, O you women, and let your ear receive the word of his mouth, and teach your daughters wailing, and everyone her neighbor lamentation. 21For death is come up into our windows, and is entered into our palaces, to cut off the children from outside, and the young men from the squares.*

One of the most important duties of the prophet in governmental intercession is to receive the plays. Then articulate the plays to the people. David is a perfect example of this. He was a king, a warrior, a worshipper, but people tend to forget he was also a prophet. That is one of the reasons why David had the type of supernatural victory he enjoyed. How many kings in history can boast like David and say they won every war? David always inquired of the

Lord. He always waited for the Lord to give him strategy and he always had success.

Prayer ministries benefit when prophets lead them. In corporate intercession, prophets do the same as the rudder of the ship. They steer. The rudder is not large, it's small, minute in comparison to the whole ship. Jeremiah said call for the wailing women and call for the skillful women. They will weep over you until they birth true travail in everybody. That's someone who understands the methodology of prayer. He's got a heavenly playbook in his hand and he knows instinctually what God wants.

The mature prophet stands at the command of the prayer army and determines what God wants based upon the intel received. They don't have to receive all intel. Their job is to determine what God wants based on the revelation received. I stand as a prophet over the prayer team in my church. People see, hear, smell all kinds of things in prayer. I'm never intimated by what our intercessors see. My job is not to see everything. My job is to make sure revelation is properly interpreted and applied.

## 2 Kings 5: 9-11

*So Naaman went with his horses and chariots and stopped at the door of Elisha's house. 10Elisha sent a messenger to say to him, "Go, wash yourself seven times in the Jordan, and your flesh will be restored and you will be cleansed." 11But Naaman went away angry and said, "I thought that he would surely come out to me and stand and call on the name of the Lord his God, wave his hand over the spot and cure me of my leprosy.*

Naaman was big time. A foreign dignitary. He was the commander of the army of Syria. Other than the king himself, no one greater could have showed up on Elisha's doorstep. Yet when Naaman comes to see the prophet, Elisha doesn't even come out to meet him. He sends a servant. Naaman is offended by this and almost misses his blessing. Prophets have to be sensitive to the move of the Spirit. They have to know when God wants them to be on center stage and when He wants them to move out of the way. Don't let people turn your gift into *Showtime at the Apollo.*

# Ezekiel 4:1-8

*"Now, son of man, take a block of clay, put it in front of you and draw the city of Jerusalem on it. 2Then lay siege to it: Erect siege works against it, build a ramp up to it, set up camps against it and put battering rams around it. 3Then take an iron pan, place it as an iron wall between you and the city and turn your face toward it. It will be under siege, and you shall besiege it. This will be a sign to the people of Israel. 4"Then lie on your left side and put the sin of the people of Israel upon yourself. You are to bear*

*their sin for the number of days you lie on your side. 5I have assigned you the same number of days as the years of their sin. So for 390 days you will bear the sin of the people of Israel. 6 "After you have finished this, lie down again, this time on your right side, and bear the sin of the people of Judah. I have assigned you 40 days, a day for each year. 7Turn your face toward the siege of Jerusalem and with bared arm prophesy against her. 8I will tie you up with ropes so that you cannot turn from one side to the other until you have finished the days of your siege.*

Another thing prophets do in prayer is to lay siege. In the above passage you have a detailed account of what God told Ezekiel to do prophetically in order to lay the siege. What is a siege? It's the act or process of surrounding and attacking a fortified place in such a way as to keep it from getting additional aid or supplies. The purpose of the siege is to lessen the resistance of the defenders and thereby make capture possible. Laying a spiritual siege is not easy. It requires some type of prolonged rigorous action. God told Ezekiel to lay on his left side for 390 days then to flip over and lay on his right side for 40 days. I guarantee you that laying on his side might not have seemed like such a bad idea for maybe that first hour or so. But for 430 days? That's more than a year. Ezekiel had to be willing to give his life to the siege. You can't go to work when you're lying on your side. I'm sure there where many days when he thought he was going to die.

Some years ago, the church that I attend wanted to build an addition on the current structure, with the goal being to expand their capacity and reach more people for Christ. The Lord spoke to my heart and said, "The people want to build. I want them to build, but spiritually you don't have the capacity to do this. The water level of intercession is too low in this house so I want you to lay a siege." My response to this? Nothing, you can hear the sound of me gulping air. Why? Because as I said before, you have to give your whole life to a siege.

He told Ezekiel to lay on his side for 430 days. What in the world would he tell me to do? He said, "Don't worry. This is a siege that I know you can do. I want you to gather the praying people and come to the church every morning between the hours of 3AM and 6AM for the entire month of October. I want you to bombard Heaven with prayer for 31 days." It was hard, but we did it. After the 31 days were up, God spoke to my heart again and said, "Now, you have to keep the ground. Choose one day where you come from 3-6AM and you pray?" This time my question was, "Well, for how long?" His response, "Until I tell you to quit."

That was 13 years ago. We still pray every Friday morning at our church, from 3-6AM at the 4$^{th}$ Watch of the morning. As for the building. We prayed for six years, the building went up in the 7$^{th}$ year and it more then doubled the previous edifice's size.

## 2 Kings 2: 19-22

*The people of the city said to Elisha, "Look, our lord, this town is well situated, as you can see, but the water is bad and the land is unproductive." 20 "Bring me a new bowl," he said, "and put salt in it." So they brought it to him. 21 Then he went out to the spring and threw the salt into it, saying, "This is what the Lord says: 'I have healed this water. Never again will it cause death or make the land unproductive.'" 22 And the water has remained pure to this day, according to the word Elisha had spoken.*

Elisha threw the salt in the water and the waters became clean. This is what you call a prophetic act. In times of corporate prayer when the Spirit is moving, prophets should do prophetic acts. However, let me qualify that statement by saying that you don't have to be a prophet in order to do a prophetic act. You just have to have prophetic insight. Scripture tells us that the water remains clean to this day. A prophetic act is something that appears to be foolish, it's done by faith, and it has lifelong implications.

†

# CHAPTER NINE
# INTIMACY & AUTHORITY

## Matthew 25:1-13

*At that time the kingdom of heaven will be like ten virgins who took their lamps and went out to meet the bridegroom. 2Five of them were foolish and five were wise. 3The foolish ones took their lamps but did not take any oil with them. 4The wise ones, however, took oil in jars along with their lamps. 5The bridegroom was a long time in coming, and they all became drowsy and fell asleep. 6"At midnight the cry rang out: 'Here's the bridegroom! Come out to meet him!' 7"Then all the virgins woke up and trimmed their lamps. 8The foolish ones said to the wise, 'Give us some of your oil; our lamps are going out.' 9" 'No,' they replied, 'there may not be enough for both us and you. Instead, go to those who sell oil and buy some for yourselves.' 10"But while they were on their way to buy the oil, the bridegroom arrived. The virgins who were ready went in with him to the wedding banquet. And the door was shut. 11"Later the others also came. 'Lord, Lord,' they said, 'open the door for us!' 12"But he replied, 'Truly I tell you, I don't know you.' 13"Therefore keep watch, because you do not know the day or the hour.*

## Luke 12:35-40

*[35] "Be dressed ready for service and keep your lamps burning, [36] like servants waiting for their master to return from a wedding banquet, so that when he comes and knocks they can immediately open the door for him. [37] It will be good for those servants whose master finds them watching when he comes. Truly I tell you, he will dress himself to serve, will have them recline at the table and will come and wait on them. [38] It will be good for those servants whose master finds them ready, even if he comes in the middle of the night or toward daybreak. [39] But understand this: If the owner of the house had known at what hour the thief was coming, he would not have let his house be broken into. [40] You also must be ready, because the Son of Man will come at an hour when you do not expect him."*

## Luke 5:15-16

*Yet the news about him spread all the more, so that crowds of people came to hear him and to be healed of their sicknesses. 16But Jesus often withdrew to lonely places and prayed.*

## Psalms 23:5

*You prepare a table for me in the presence of my enemies, you anoint my head with oil, my cup overflows.*

Say this with me: God wants me to minister from my overflow. If you rise to meet Him whenever He calls you. Even if He calls you in the middle of the night, You will always have oil. Your lamp will always be filled. You will minister to people out of your overflow. Not from your personal stock but from your overflow.

Ministering to the people is a lot like carrying a baby. When you are pregnant they tell you that you have to take the prenatal pills. So that the baby can get what it needs, but also, for another very important reason: so the baby does not began to pull strength from your bones. You'll find yourself dry and brittle and eventually broken if you allow the people of God to draw strength from your bones. Jesus understood this that's why He went away to be with the Father every chance He got. The more His ministry started to 'blow up' the more He went away to solidary places to pray.

## Matthew 7:21-23

*"Not everyone who says to me, 'Lord, Lord,' will enter the kingdom of heaven, but only the one who does the will of my Father who is in heaven. $^{22}$ Many*

*will say to me on that day, 'Lord, Lord, did we not prophesy in your name and in your name drive out demons and in your name perform many miracles?' $^{23}$ Then I will tell them plainly, 'I never knew you. Away from me, you evildoers!'*

This is the scariest passage in the Bible to me. These are not some fly by night Christians. These are people with real power. Yet somewhere along the line they missed the boat. Here's what I think happened, they grew in authority but not in intimacy. So much so that the Father could turn around and tell them on that Great Day, depart from me I never knew you. I've pondered this verse for a long time and wondered how it could possibly happen. I've come to the conclusion that we are all prone to fall into the same trap that Satan fell into. Deceived by the power of God. It is an amazing thing to feel the power of God coursing through you.

It's easy to be deceived and think that, because God is using us that means that He is for us. It becomes easy for us to sin and then get back up and minister because we feel His anointing upon us when we are ministering to His people, We begin to say things like, "God knows my heart. He knows I'm not perfect. Everything is copasetic." If you've ever felt the power of God move in and through you, I'm telling you, it's easy to buy into the doctrine of devils that says, "Once saved always saved, I can't lose my salvation." According to Ezekiel 44 that's not true.

# Ezekiel 44:10-16

*10" 'The Levites who went far from me when Israel went astray and who wandered from me after their idols must bear the consequences of their sin. 11They may serve in my sanctuary, having charge of the gates of the temple and serving in it; they may slaughter the burnt offerings and sacrifices for the people and stand before the people and serve them. 12But because they served them in the presence of their idols and made the people of Israel fall into sin, therefore I have sworn with uplifted hand that they must bear the consequences of their sin, declares the Sovereign Lord. 13They are not to come near to serve me as priests or come near any of my holy things or my most holy offerings; they must bear the shame of their detestable practices. 14And I will appoint them to guard the temple for all the work that is to be done in it. 15" 'But the Levitical priests, who are descendants of Zadok and who guarded my sanctuary when the Israelites went astray from me, are to come near to minister before me; they are to stand before me to offer sacrifices of fat and blood, declares the Sovereign Lord. 16They alone are to enter my sanctuary; they alone are to come near my table to minister before me and serve me as guards.*

According to Ezekiel 44, it's possible for God to still use you and be done with you. He made a distinction in His Word between the Levites, between those who taught the people right from wrong, and those who caused the people to fall into sin. He says, I know I'm going to always have both of these kinds in my camp.

But here's what I'm going to do. I'm going to let them serve me. I'm going to let them take care of my house. They're going to lead the people into worship. They will lay hands on the sick and watch them recover. They're going to perform all the priestly duties assigned to them. But I'll never let them come near me. I will never be intimate with them. And when they take their last breath they will have led millions into the kingdom but they will bust Hell wide open. That's the curse. My earnest prayer today is O' Lord please don't ever let that curse befall me nor any of the readers of this book.

## 1 Peter 1:15-16

*but like the Holy One who called you, be holy yourselves also in all your behavior; **16**because it is written, "YOU SHALL BE HOLY, FOR I AM HOLY*

## Romans 13:12-13

*$^{12}$ The night is nearly over; the day is almost here. So let us put aside the deeds of darkness and put on the armor of light. $^{13}$ Let us behave decently, as in the daytime, not in carousing and drunkenness, not in sexual immorality and debauchery, not in dissension and jealousy.*

In the past I've always felt uncomfortable about adding those two scriptures to this course. I used to think, that since we are talking about prayer, holiness should be a given. Seemed like a no-brainer to me. But after watching so many people live a life of practiced sin and move powerfully in God, I now realize that this must be said. Be Holy even as your God is Holy. Intercessors ought to repent often and keep a short list before God. It's not the big things that get us, it's usually the small foxes. Just as the Biblical priests were set apart for God's service, so we also need to be set apart. I can't lay my eyes on everything and still think I can see in the spirit. I can't cuss my family out in one breath and think I can prophesy in the next. I can't just listen to anything I want to. I need to show regard to the resident member of the Godhead who lives inside of me.

## Luke 10:38-41

*[38] As Jesus and his disciples were on their way, he came to a village where a woman named Martha opened her home to him. [39] She had a sister called Mary, who sat at the Lord's feet listening to what he said. [40] But Martha was distracted by all the preparations that had to be made. She came to him and asked, "Lord, don't you care that my sister has left me to do the work by myself? Tell her to help me!" Martha, Martha you are worried and upset about many things but only one thing is needed. Mary has chosen what is better and it will not be taken away from her.*

We know the scripture that tells us that His ways are higher than our ways and that His thoughts are not our thoughts (Isaiah 55:8-9). We quote that a lot right? What we don't say, is that most times, God's way of thinking is fundamentally opposite to human thinking. For example, let's take this statement Mary has chosen the better portion. What does it mean that Mary has chosen the better portion? Martha's working hard for the kingdom, she's frying the chicken, providing sustenance for Jesus's natural body, but yet He says that Mary has chosen the better portion.

In the church world today, we take this stance that the out-front ministry is the better portion, but it is not. It may be the thing that brings us accolades, the pats on the back, and the that-a-boy or that-a-girl, but Jesus said that Mary chose the better portion. Our thinking is paradoxically different from God's. Mary is doing the thing that Mankind was created to do in the first place. Shoot the breeze with God. People try and work hard to get to the next level of authority. Work hard in school, work hard on the job to get that next promotion. But authority comes through relationship. The real deals are made after work hours, while people form bonds of intimacy with each other. So it is with God. Here's the 9th and final principle I'm going to give you in this book:

# PRINCIPLE # 9

## IT'S NOT ENOUGH TO GROW IN AUTHORITY IN HIM, YOU MUST ALSO GROW IN INTIMACY WITH HIM.

God doesn't just look at your track record of service and decide to promote you. God says, "Does he know me? Do I know him? How much time have they spent off the clock with me? Just because you work for me, that doesn't make us friends." The main point I want to convey to you is that: if you haven't done so already, please become God's friend. And if you haven't been a good friend, take some serious time off of your kingdom work and fix the relationship.

Any husband and wife team will tell you that the relationship will start to go downhill quickly, if once they go into business together, all they ever talk about is business. If we don't take the time to cultivate our personal relationship this will not be a very good relationship for very long. That's worth taking some time away from ministry to do that. You want to grow like an oak not a watermelon. You want to be solid thru and thru. Intimacy with the Creator is the only way to do that.

# INVITATION TO JOIN THE FAMILY OF GOD

I hope you enjoyed this study on prayer and intercession, perhaps your reading this because you are curious, but you haven't made a commitment to follow Christ. If you have not already done so, I would like to invite you to become a member of the family of God. If you would like to make Jesus Christ the Lord of your life, simply pray the following prayer with me:

Dear Jesus, I am fully convinced that you are God. That you shed your divinity and came to Earth and lived as a human for the purpose of redeeming me. I believe you died on the cross and rose again. I accept you as the only valid Lord and King over my life and I pledge my allegiance to you. I invite you to come into my life and transform me, and to make me a vessel suitable for your use.

Beloved, if you just prayed that prayer you've just received the free, and yet very costly, gift of salvation. All of Heaven is rejoicing right now over you. Welcome to the Kingdom of God. May you do awesome business with, for and on behalf of our Matchless King.

# ABOUT THE AUTHOR

Catrina J. Sparkman is a licensed, ordained minister and the founder of The Ironer's Press which hosts Prayer Parties, a seasonal gathering of intercessors from all over the Midwest, as well as The Fourth Watch, a 3-6AM prayer meeting, that happens every Friday morning in her home city.

She is the author of various works of fiction and non-fiction. An inspirational speaker, consultant, presenter, and personal empowerment coach, for various churches and ministry organizations, Catrina teaches on prayer, the prophetic ministry, and healing. She lives in Madison, WI with her husband, Wesley, and their three beautiful children.

She can be reached at:
doingbusinesswithgod@gmail.com

www.ingramcontent.com/pod-product-compliance
Lightning Source LLC
Chambersburg PA
CBHW020139130526
44591CB00030B/152